THE
OL' BALL GAME

THE OL' BALL GAME

A COLLECTION OF BASEBALL CHARACTERS AND MOMENTS WORTH REMEMBERING

BARNES
&NOBLE
BOOKS
NEW YORK

This edition published by Barnes & Noble, Inc.,
by arrangement with Stackpole Books.

1993 Barnes & Noble Books

ISBN 1-56619-058-4

Printed and bound in the United States of America

M 9 8 7 6 5 4 3

Our thanks to John Duxbury,
"The Answer Man,"
for his invaluable assistance
and his methodical fact-checking.
—The Editors

CONTENTS

(continued)

OLD HOSS

Peter Wallan

CHARLES RADBOURN'S BRONZE plaque in the Baseball Hall of Fame in Cooperstown, New York calls him "the greatest of all 19th century pitchers—winner of 309 major league games between 1880 and 1891." But it was just a part of one of those years—the late summer of 1884—that made Radbourn a legend.

Sure, Charlie Radbourn won 31 and 49 games for the Providence Grays of the National League in 1882 and 1883, but that was no big deal in the era of the two-man pitching staffs. Why, in 1883 alone, Grasshopper Jim Whitney of Boston, Larry Corcoran of Cap Anson's Chicago White Stockings and Pud Galvin of Buffalo had topped 30 wins. Even Stump Weidman of the woeful Detroit Wolverines managed 20 victories that year, and Stump once lost 36 games in a single season.

After enduring a third place finish behind the champion Boston Beaneaters in 1883, Providence fans were confident in the spring of 1884. The strong-armed Radbourn was back and manager Frank Bancroft had secured the services of a young and brash tyro from the West Coast to help Charlie "at the points." Twenty-one year old right-hander Charlie Sweeney, who had the proverbial cup of coffee with the Grays in 1883, pronounced himself "ready and raring to go" as the season commenced. Heck, with Sweeney and Radbourn alternating on the mound, what could possibly befall manager Bancroft and his doughty crew of young men?

Unfortunately, Sweeney was "raring to go" for much more than just baseball. After spending the greater part of May and June sampling the varied delights of the city of Providence by gaslight, Sweeney began to get on Radbourn's nerves. This was no mean feat, either, since the worldly Radbourn was one of 20 children, had bounced through remote baseball outposts as Dubuque, Peoria and Bloomington, and was certainly not above dabbling in questionable social extra-curricular activities himself.

The animosity between the two deepened. By late July, the big (and usually hung-over) Californian had somehow managed a 17-8 record and Charlie Radbourn was in a deep sulk. The situation came to a head on July 16 when Radbourn took the mound against Boston and lost 5-2, pitching with "reackless haste and wild abandon" and "attempting to break up catcher Barney Gilligan by throwing fast balls when poor little Barney was expecting curves."

Bancroft was "utterly disgusted with the exhibition of puerile peevishness by one Charles Radbourn" and hot-tempered Charlie was summarily brought before the sullen Providence Grays Board of Directors to answer "certain pungent conundrums touching his peculiar conduct of the past three weeks."

After all the weighty words were digested, the seething Bancroft suspended his 49-game winner without pay and told Sweeney that he would be the Grays main man for the rest of the season.

But the heavy mantle of responsibility rested awkwardly on Charlie's broad shoulders. Sweeney immediately went on one of his several monumental benders (once, it took a spectacular dunking in the murky Seekonk River to put him in an acceptable mental state to pitch) and the disgusted Bancroft had seen more than enough. Told to shape up or ship out, the red-eyed Sweeney opted for the latter, entraining for St. Louis on July 23 where he joined that city's team in the then major but 'outlaw' Union Association.

Now the Providence Grays were left with no pitchers—or were they?

"Do you want to win the pennant?" Radbourn asked Bancroft.

"Damn right," Bancroft answered.

"Then let me pitch all the rest of the games."

With the Grays trailing Boston by one game, Bancroft had no choice but to agree to Radbourn's preposterous idea. It seemed a thoroughly impossible task but the stubborn 5'9", 170-pound Radbourn did have one advantage. Despite rule changes that permitted overhand pitching for 1884, Charlie stuck to his old-fashioned method of throwing underhanded. What he gave up in speed he gained in control—and endurance. Charlie, of course, wanted a bit more in the way of recompense for his proposed overtime. The parsimonious Providence Grays Board of Directors, after a hasty meeting, forked it over wihout even fluttering an eyelash.

Legend has it that Radbourn won all the remaining Grays games. He did not—just most of them. Providence played 30 times between July 23 and September 21 and Charlie won 26 of 28 starts, 18 in succession. One of his losses came when third baseman Jerry Denny botched a ground ball to give the New York Giants a 2-1, 11-inning victory. In the other, he was outpitched 2-0 by Buffalo Hall-of-Famer Pud Galvin. Amateur "change pitchers" Joe (Cyclone) Miller and Ed Conley, a Woonsocket, Rhode Island teenager, won the other two games against weak teams.

Radbourn reached his pinnacle during a crucial four-game series with the powerful defending champion Boston Beaneaters. He opened festivities with a spectacular 12 strikeout, 1-0 whitewashing of Boston ace Charlie Buffington. The game was scoreless until the 11th inning when Grays shortstop Art Irwin lined a rare home run through a hole in a temporary fence at Boston's South End Grounds, sending 6,027 Hub fans into a state of near-apoplexy. The Grays took the next two games behind Radbourn, 3-1 and 4-0, and then Buffington again strode to the mound to challenge Providence's rubber-armed wonder.

The result was exactly the same. The game was tense and scoreless through seven innings but Barney Gilligan walked to open the Grays eighth. He was forced by Paul Radford, who promptly moved to second when Boston catcher Mert Hackett treated one of Buffington's tricky overhand hummers like a poisonous reptile. Paul Hines then slashed a game-winning single to center, giving the Grays an insurmountable five-game lead in the National League standings and Charlie Radbourn his eternal nickname—Old Hoss.

And how the Providence fans loved their 'Charlie.' With the Grays first pennant since 1879 almost a foregone conclusion, Old Hoss didn't let up one iota. On September 2 he outpitched Buffalo's Galvin 4-0 before a doting home crowd. After the game he was presented with a handsome crayon portrait of himself—in a gold frame, no less.

One week later, Old Hoss fanned 12 Cleveland batters in a 9-1 victory that moved one commenter to gush, ". . . despite its recent efforts, Radbourn's strong arm has not forgotten its cunning. . . ." (The gallivanting Old Hoss's inspiring performance, though, may have had something to do with a novel promotion staged by the Grays management—it was Lady's Day.)

Three days later, in the last home game of the season, the Grays rode Charlie's untiring arm to a 6-1 victory over Philadelphia, after which he was presented with a "huge envelope bursting with lawful currency of the United States." The cascade of victories had apparently washed away all bitter memories of Old Hoss's earlier "puerile peevishness."

With the pennant safely in the satchel, Old Hoss rested, taking a week off before beating Philadelphia again 8-0 in the season finale, making the Grays' margin over second-place Boston 10½ games. It was Charlie's 60th win against 12 losses. He had worked an implausible 679 innings, struck out 411 (it took four strikes to retire a batter in 1884), pitched 11 shutouts, and recorded an ERA of 1.38. He also batted cleanup.

There was one more challenge, though.

Garrulous Jim Murtrie's New York Metropolitans of the rival American Association were making shrill noises to the effect that they were the best team in baseball. The Grays traveled to the frigid Polo Grounds in New York City in late October and ended Murtrie's dream in a three-game sweep behind—who else?—Old Hoss.

So dominating was Radbourn that star Metropolitan pitcher Tim Keefe, a loser in the first two games, volunteered to umpire the third "just so I can get a look at this man close up." The Mets' 37-game winner got an eyeful and then some. Providence won 11-2 and returned home with their coveted prize—a $100 embroidered silk pennant.

The champion Grays were magnanimous in victory, giving their valuable Old Hoss a $2,000 raise for the 1885 season. With a young team and their mound problems solved, there was no telling how many more pennants would fly proudly over the little Messer Street Grounds in Providence.

Alas, what they didn't know was that, at age 31, Charlie Radbourn's gallant arm had gone stone dead.

Radbourn was just 26-20 in 1885 and Providence slipped to fourth place. By November, the once-proud Grays were no more—the franchise was disbanded and Old Hoss trundled sadly off to arch-rival Boston, pitching with only moderate success. In 1890, he did manage to pace Mike (King) Kelley's Boston Player's League team to a championship, but it was to be his last hurrah. Ravaged by the effects of syphilis, he struggled to a 12-12 record with Cincinatti in 1891 and then became too weak to continue pitching.

Radbourn meandered back to his native Bloomington, Illinois to open a pool hall and sporting bar but quickly found that his luck had gone as lame as his once indestructable right arm. Horribly mangled and partially paralyzed in a hunting accident in 1894, he died a lonely recluse in Bloomington on February 5, 1897 at the age of 43.

And what of his old nemesis, Charlie Sweeney?

Sweeney's raw talent racked up 41 victories for Providence and St. Louis, but his rough-hewn command of life in no way matched his mastery of a baseball. Sentenced to San Quentin Prison for first-degree murder, he was himself shot and killed during a prison altercation in 1902.

Baseball records come and go. They are, of course, made to be broken. Babe Ruth's once mystical "60" is gone—or at least unceremoniously shunted aside by a cold asterisk. Charlie Radbourn's mark of "60" may be the only baseball record that will stand alone forever.

The remarkable Old Hoss should be very proud. Wherever he is.

BATS AND BAYONETS

Michael Morgan

TODAY, HISTORIANS DISMISS the notion that baseball was invented by Abner Doubleday. Instead, they point to a variety of games, such as town ball, stool ball, and rounders, as the ancestors of baseball. By the beginning of the Civil War, baseball had virtually completed its evolution and closely resembled the modern game. Organized baseball clubs had appeared by the 1840s, regular games were played by the 1850s, and intercity play had begun before the outbreak of the Civil War. The young men who went off to fight took baseball with them and played whenever the opportunity arose.

When the men of the 165th New York landed on Hilton Head Island near the mouth of the Savannah River on December 22, 1862, they were eager to meet the rebels in battle. But the sea islands in that area had already been secured by other Union troops. With no Confederates to fight, the Union soldiers quickly organized a friendly combat of their own: a game of baseball. On Christmas Day, the 165th played the 48th New York in a game witnessed by as many as 10,000 spectators. Although no one present bothered to record the score, the game made a deep impression on those who witnessed it. As the years passed, the size of the crowd grew in the memory of the onlookers from 10,000 to 40,000 people. Baseball had arrived as a spectator sport.

Many of the ball-playing soldiers were city boys who knew little about life in the field. When the greenhorns of the 79th New York wrestled with setting up their tents, they gave up in disgust. They played a game of baseball until more experienced hands arrived to show them the intricacies of setting up a ridgepole. As their regimental historian put it: "It was rather a difficult undertaking for the majority of us, this pitching tents—we could pitch ball better."

The Christmas Day game was not the only time troops on the sea islands put down the musket and bayonet and picked up the bat and ball. When the 71st New York Volunteers reached Washington, D.C., in the days of the war, they received a challenge from local baseball enthusiasts. Playing nearly in the shadow of the White House, the 71st defeated the Washington team 42–13. Shortly thereafter, the 71st marched out of the capital to meet the Confederates at Bull Run, where it sustained heavy casualties.

Major battles, such as Bull Run, were important but rare occurrences. Most of the soldiers' days were spent drilling, marching, and doing housekeeping chores. Baseball offered a refreshing break from the tedium of camp life. Once the coastal islands were cleared of Confederates, there was little for the Union troops to do. There were so many baseball games that one eyewitness commented: "Baseball has become a regular institution in which the whole garrison joined, from the colonel down."

Another break from camp routine was the arrival of a photographer to take formal pictures of the troops. The soldiers did not let such an occasion pass without the inclusion of their baseball activities. Although baseball was not the focus of a formal photograph at Fort Pulaski, some troops carefully arranged themselves in ball-playing poses in the background while Company G of the 48th New York was photographed in the foreground.

Another secure area during the middle years of the Civil War was the area around Hampton Roads. Here too a large number of Union soldiers found enough leisure time to play baseball. Teams were organized along regimental lines and games were played in the afternoon, between drill and dress parade. A regimental rivalry was sparked between the 9th and 51st New York regiments. During a series of games in March, 1862, the Zouaves of the 9th were nearly always victorious. At the end of each game, the men of the winning 9th taunted the losing 51st with a barrage of verbal insults. The men of the 9th wondered aloud, after a string of victories, if there were any other game the 51st could play better than baseball.

At the same time, a member of the 13th New Hampshire reported that nearly every company in the Newport News area was playing baseball. There seemed to be hundreds of games going on at the same time. For many of these young players, the game served as a revival of their school days and a cure for homesickness.

Soldiers enlivened their games with a few friendly wagers. In early 1863, the 19th Massachusetts defeated the 7th Michigan and won a prize of $120. On this occasion, the money was spent to treat both teams to dinner. As one soldier said, "It was a grand time, and all agreed it was nicer to play base than minie ball."

The 20th Wisconsin, like their eastern counterparts, became bored with camp life. A baseball game was organized between wings of the regiment for a prize of $25. The right wing won the game—and the money—by outscoring the left wing by eight runs.

Although Southerners played baseball, their recollections were not as detailed as those recorded by the Northern troops. One Confederate did remember a match game between the Confederate Baseball Club and the Southern Baseball Club. In the first inning, the Confederates scored three times while shutting the Southerners out in their half of the inning. The Confederates maintained their lead until the fifth, when the Southerners came from behind to take the lead and the game. The final score was 19–11 in favor of the Southern Club. As in the Union army, gambling seemed to be a universal habit: "Among sporting characters a considerable amount of money changed hands."

Even when captured, troops from both sides continued to play baseball. The commander of Fort McHenry in Baltimore, Maryland, was criticized for the poor treatment of captured Confederates in his care. "I am told that they did not hesitate to express satisfaction with their treatment," he pleaded defensively. "They appeared to enjoy their daily game of ball greatly."

When the war ended and the troops returned home, they remembered the ball games they had seen and played during the war. In the wave of interest in baseball that followed, Civil War veterans composed the heart of many teams. Far more former soldiers, however, followed the example of the Christmas Day game on Hilton Head Island and turned out to watch the newly organized teams. Baseball as a professional spectator sport had become part of the American social fabric.

Young Art's Invention

Norman L. Macht

THERE'S ONLY ONE pitcher in the Baseball Hall of Fame who lost more games in the major leagues than he won. William Arthur "Candy" Cummings was elected to the Pioneers department in 1939 not for his record, but because of what he invented—the curveball.

Born in Ware, Massachusetts October 17, 1848, Cummings grew up in a time when pitchers delivered the ball underhand. He was a slender, wiry young man, never topping 5′9″ or 120 pounds. But he had unusually long, thin arms that he would curl up and snap like a whip. He moved to Brooklyn as a teenager, and it was there he set about developing the "outcurve," as it was first called.

There have been many versions of how and when he discovered—or invented—the pitch. In the following letter, written in 1896 at 26 Pleasant Street, Brooklyn, he set the record straight.

"You want to know how I discovered the curve and if it was accidental. Well, I will tell you just how I got it. In regard to its being an accident, it was not. But it was hard work and studying out a theory I had.

"Possibly you have thrown clam shells and have seen how they would sail through the air then turn, whether to the right or left, as the wind happened to strike them. A number of my chums and I were throwing shells one day in Brooklyn. When seeing a shell take a wide curve I said, 'Now, if I could only make the ball do that I think the other clubs won't be in it.' There was immediately a discussion on the art and possibilities of curving the ball, all hands insisting it was an impossible thing. I took the opposite side of the question and said it could be done. I told them I was going to do it if it took me ten years. This was in '64 when I was in my 16th year.

"I commenced thinking and puzzling my brain as to how I was to accomplish it, and it was a constant study and lots of hard work. It was very discouraging too, I can assure you. At times I would think I had it, and the boys would get behind my catcher and sometimes they would think they saw it and others would say that it came straight. They chaffed me so much I decided to say nothing to them but worked quietly until I got it. I went back to boarding school that fall and every minute I had away from study and recitations I put to pitching. Still I was not sure of it. After I left school in the fall of '65 I still kept up working on the one thing. In the meantime I found I could pitch a raise or a drop ball and felt quite encouraged, and I determined to stick to it until I got it.

"In the summer of '66 I joined the Excelsior club of Brooklyn as a junior member and pitching for the second nine, pitching a few games on the first nine and won them, much to the surprise of our opponents. In the fall of '66 or '67, I'm not positive which, we went to Boston to play the Lowells, Tri-Mountains and Harvards, and I then found that I had got what I had been working for. While we were playing the Harvards, I pitched a ball at Archie Bush, and I thought he would bat it out of sight, when, as he struck at the ball, it seemed to go about a foot beyond the end of his bat. I tried again with the same result, and I was then sure I had the curve and have been able to hold onto it ever since.

"It was no easy job for a pitcher to deliver a ball in those days, as he had to keep both feet on the ground and not raise either until after the ball left his hand, and had to keep his arm close to his side and deliver the ball with a perpendicular swing. I think if some of the boys tried it they would find it a difficult thing to do, and you must make your wrist and second finger do all the work. It is very trying to the wrist, as the snap you give the ball, similar to snapping a whip, has a tendency to throw your wrist bone out of place, as I have done mine hundreds of times. In 1874 in Philadelphia my wrist bone was out so I had to wear a rubber supporter all that season."

/s/ W. A. Cummings

A graceful, confident player, Cummings was known as a boy wonder among amateur baseball circles, and a nemesis to the heavy hitters of the time. He won 16 and lost 8 for Hartford in the National League in 1876, and was 5-14 at Cincinnati in '77. Cummings was also the first pitcher to use the inshoot, the raise, the drop and the double curve—the snake ball— that curved almost to the plate then broke sharply the other way. He was always willing to teach others how to curve the ball, and worked with pitchers at Princeton and Yale in the 1870s. One of his students was Joseph McElroy Mann, who used the curve in pitching the first recorded no-hitter, pitching for Princeton against Yale at New Haven on May 29, 1875.

Cummings owned a paint and wallpaper store in Atholl, Massachusetts, when his playing days were over, returning to Brooklyn when his wife died in 1895. He died May 16, 1924, in Toledo, Ohio.

WILHOIT, THE WICHITA WONDER

Bill Rabinowitz

Things weren't exactly looking up for Joe Wilhoit as he got set to play for the Wichita Witches on June 14, 1919. After playing parts of the last three seasons with the Boston Braves, Pittsburgh Pirates, and National League champion New York Giants, the 27-year-old Wilhoit found himself back in the minors playing in the Class-A Western League, struggling to keep his average above .200. Wilhoit seemed destined for oblivion. Little could he or anyone else have known that his infield hit leading off the Wichita first inning would be the genesis of an amazing streak that would remain, to this day, professional baseball's longest.

The infield single was Wilhoit's only hit June 14, but the next day he began a torrid 12-game multi-hit string. Wilhoit collected three hits in the first game of a doubleheader against Oklahoma City, including the game-winner in the bottom of the ninth inning, and had two singles in the nightcap.

The left-handed-hitting Wilhoit followed with three 2-hit games, and 3-for-4, and 5-for-8 doubleheader against Des Moines and three more 2-hit games. In the 12 games, Joe hit .510 (25-for-49). He would keep up that pace for almost two more months.

What sparked Wilhoit's hot bat? The Wichita *Eagle* newspaper never suggested any theory, and because sportswriters back then didn't venture out of the press box to interview players, it's impossible to know if Wilhoit had an explanation.

Sec Taylor, a Des Moines *Register* sports columnist, wrote in 1933 (during Joe DiMaggio's 61-game minor-league streak) that Wilhoit's tear began shortly after switching bats. According to Taylor, when a struggling Wilhoit was acquired in a May 19 trade with Seattle of the Pacific Coast

League, he had been using a heavy, thick-handled bat. When Wilhoit continued to slump with Wichita, Witches manager (and owner) Frank Isbell persuaded him to try a lighter, smaller-handled bat. That apparently did the trick.

On June 29, 1919, the *Eagle* first mentioned Wilhoit's streak which by then had reached 15 games.

"The work of Wilhoit in center field has been the feature of the games here," the paper reported. "The big gardener has boosted his average to .336 and threatens to take the lead in the league."

June 29 also was the day Wilhoit had his first close call. But after being hitless in three at bats in the opener of a doubleheader, Joe came through with a single. Four games later, Wilhoit faced the same situation. Once again, he responded with an eighth-inning single.

Game after game, his streak continued. But while the Western League pitchers were unable to stop Wilhoit, other forces threatened to. On July 11, with the streak at 29, the *Eagle* reported that Isbell had received numerous offers from major-league clubs for Wilhoit. If Isbell sold or traded his star, the streak would be over.

The *Eagle* speculated on July 17 that "it is too much to hope that he [Wilhoit] will remain in these parts long." But evidently, Isbell wasn't satisfied with the offers for Wilhoit. Isbell realized that he had one hot gate attraction as long as the streak lasted. In addition, Wilhoit's exploits had led the Witches out of the cellar and into contention for the league lead.

On July 22, the streak hit 40, equalling Ty Cobb's major-league record (not counting Wee Willie Keeler's premodern 44-game streak) and five short of the professional mark set by Jack Ness for Oakland (PCL) in 1915.

"Wilhoit's great work is so extraordinary," proclaimed the *Eagle* that day, "that it is that chief topic among local fans and has attracted attention all over the circuit."

Wilhoit ripped five hits on July 23, three each the next two days, and beat out a first-inning infield hit on the 26th.

An overflow crowd of more than 4600 fans, the largest of the season, showed up at Island Park to see Wilhoit go for the record in a doubleheader against Tulsa on the 27th.

They would not be disappointed. Wilhoit tied Ness's mark with a bunt single down the third-base line in the opener and wasted no time breaking the record in the nightcap. On the first pitch in the Wichita first inning, Wilhoit cracked a double to center field, one of four hits he would get in the game.

To show appreciation of their star, the Wichita fans showered the field with money. They didn't stop until about $500 (accounts vary) was collected and given to Wilhoit, quite a sum considering that the average Class-A player then earned less than $200 a month.

"The great man refused to make a speech, proving that he is a great ballplayer," the *Eagle* proclaimed. ". . . Joe is not a pugnacious player. He takes things easy and the fans, players and umps delight in praising his work."

After Wilhoit continued the streak with a triple on the 28th, he and his Wichita teammates began a three-week road trip. By now, the streak was getting national attention. "Every paper in the country that has a sports column had run a story of Joe's feat," the *Eagle* said. "Joe . . . is the biggest little advertisement the town has had for many a day."

The Sporting News reported in early August that, "Never, in the annals of Western League baseball has so much interest and enthusiasm been aroused among fans as has been caused by the feat of this hard-hitting outfielder. . . . The fans talked of nothing else."

And Wilhoit kept up his pace. Three hits on the 30th. Then two. Two again. Three. Two. Three. Three again.

Not until August 7th did Wilhoit find his streak in jeopardy, but he singled in his fourth at bat. For the next week, Wilhoit's streak continued routinely.

Then, in an August 14 doubleheader at Omaha, the streak, now at 61, almost ended. In the opener, Wilhoit was hitless with the score tied 3-3 going to the home ninth inning. Omaha threatened, but the Witches threw out what would have been the winning run at the plate. Wilhoit got another chance. In the eleventh, Wilhoit took advantage of his opportunity with a two-run homer to right to give the Witches the victory.

In the second game, Wilhoit was 0 for 3 when he came to the plate in the sixth with the Witches trailing 9-2. He laid down a bunt to Bert Graham. Graham usually played right field, but was playing the hot corner because of an injury to the regular third baseman.

According to the *Eagle's* account, Graham could have thrown Wilhoit out, but with his team ahead by seven runs decided to hold the ball instead. "Graham's sportsmanship drew forth the admiration of the crowd," the *Eagle* reported.

Tainted or not, the streak was still alive. But it was losing steam. Wilhoit needed last at bat singles on August 16 and 17 to keep the streak going.

After getting two hits in the next game, Wilhoit and the Witches returned for a home stand. Wilhoit hit safely in both games of a double-header on August 19 to extend the streak to 69 games.

The next day Wilhoit tried to make it 70. He grounded out sharply to short, popped up and struck out in his first three at bats against Tulsa pitcher Elam Vangilder. In his fourth at bat, Wilhoit walked with two out in the seventh off reliever Jack Knight, who was pitching under the assumed surname of Williams. Still, with Wichita trailing, 2-1, going into the last of the eighth, it appeared Wilhoit would get another chance in the ninth.

But it wasn't to be. With one out, Wichita loaded the bases on three walks. By now, Bill Bayne had relieved Williams. Ray Wolfe forced the lead runner on a grounder to first and narrowly beat out what would have been an inning-ending double play on the return throw to first.

It came down to eighth-place hitter Yam Yaryan. With two strikes, Yaryan pulled Bayne's pitch just inside the third-base line for a double, giving the Witches a 3-2 lead.

Isbell elected not to pinch-hit for pitcher Paul Musser and he made the third out (after two more runs had been scored on a wild pitch) with Wilhoit on deck. Musser retired Tulsa easily in the ninth to end the game. Joe Wilhoit's streak was over abruptly at 69 games.

During the streak, Wilhoit hit .512 (153 for 299), including 24 doubles, nine triples and five home runs. He walked 34 times. In 50 of the games, Wilhoit had two or more hits.

Isbell had sold Wilhoit to the Boston Red Sox shortly before the streak ended, though Joe played for another month with the Witches before going to Boston. In 128 games with Wichita, Wilhoit hit .422, which easily led the league.

Wilhoit played in six games with the Red Sox, hitting .333 in 18 at bats. One of the other outfielders on the team was a 24-year-old named Babe Ruth, who was on his way to hitting 29 home runs for his first of many undisputed homer titles.

Although Ruth was just getting started, Wilhoit's time with the Red Sox was the last he would spend in the major leagues. Boston released Wilhoit in February 1920. He played that year with Toledo of the American Association, hitting .300 in 104 games.

Wilhoit finished his career by spending the next three years with Salt Lake of the PCL. In 1923, Wilhoit hit .360 in 172 games. But by then, he was 32 and no longer a major-league prospect so he decided to retire. He returned to Santa Barbara, California, where he had lived since childhood. In Santa Barbara, Wilhoit operated a luggage shop which he had purchased during his playing career. He ran the shop until becoming sick in the summer of 1930. Wilhoit died September 26 after a two-month illness at the age of 38.

Today, Wilhoit is all but forgotten except by the most hardcore fans, largely because his hitting streak has not been challenged. No professional player in recent years has come close enough to his mark for the media to resurrect the amazing feat Joe Wilhoit accomplished 71 seasons ago.

SAY IT
AIN'T SO, HOD

Gary Eller

MANY YEARS AGO every crossroads community exhibited a baseball club. And though its followers were as fervent as those of today, its most skilled players labored largely in unrelieved obscurity, for the major leagues stood remote and inaccessible. Henryville, Illinois, was such a place. Here the Cincinnati Reds, managed by the saintly Christy Mathewson, scheduled an exhibition game late in 1916. Scheduled to pitch for the home team semi-pro Grays was Hod Eller.

Eller, with a will as strong as his throwing arm, began the season with Moline of the Three-I League, but was available to the Grays following his suspension over a contract dispute—not the final time in his career for such an occurrence. As a result, a problem loomed. Under the rules of organized baseball, Eller was ineligible to pitch against the Reds, a professional club. It seemed his chance must pass him by, and unfortunately so, for he'd become a local sensation, having struck out 20 batters, including 13 in a row, against Kokomo two weeks earlier.

At the last minute, league officials exchanged telegrams. The functionaries twisted the terms. Eller agreed to them, and he strode to the mound to attempt to throw a baseball past a few who could rightfully count themselves among the most skilled in the world at preventing him from doing just that. And though he lost the game 2-0, he allowed the big leaguers but four hits as he mixed his shiners with raw fastballs. His performance impressed Mathewson sufficiently that Cincinnati drafted Eller from Moline. The next April the young right-hander turned up in the ballparks of New York, Philadelphia, and other storied cities of the East wearing the distinctive baggy uniform of the Cincinnati Reds.

Although he had other pitches, Eller relied on one known today mainly to the furtive. It was the shine ball, a pitch hurlers of the era threw after rubbing or "shining" the ball on a dab on paraffin previously deposited on a convenient area of the uniform, often the pant leg. The paraffin (similar to candle wax) altered the otherwise even texture of the ball, causing it to follow an erratic path on its way to the catcher. The shine ball, known also as a "dry spitter," was in fact a cousin to the spitball. The latter, of course, became a tool relied on by many a generation of big-league pitchers.

And it was entirely legal. Several, including Eddie Cicotte, used it as their prime weapon, though Eller became its best-known upholder in his league. With the help of the pitch he managed ten wins his rookie year of 1917. On August 21 of that year, he became only the third pitcher in modern major-league history to strike out the side on the minimum nine pitches. In 1918 Eller won 16 games, including seven in a row in the war-shortened 130-game season. In July a writer in *The Sporting News* referred to him as "one of the best of all right-handers, one of the game's greatest pitchers."

The year 1919 arrived full of promise and change. The Great War had ended. The season began with the Red Sox favored to repeat in the American League, the Giants and Cubs in the National.

Although the Reds started the season indifferently, a promise of fortune appeared on May 11 when Hod Eller threw a no-hitter against the St. Louis Cardinals, led by the great Rogers Hornsby. By the season's end he'd won 20 games and finished second in the league in total strikeouts with 137. Its offense led by future Hall-of-Famer Edd Roush and Heinie Groh, the Reds took the pennant by nine games.

In the American League Boston's slump helped disencumber the way for Chicago. Although the White Sox triumphed by three and one-half games, one sportswriter felt they exhausted themselves in the pursuit of Tris Speaker and his Cleveland club. Nonetheless, and in spite of Cincinnati's superior pitching, Chicago became the early favorite among betters, mostly on the strength of their World Series experience. Not until the day of the first game of the expanded best-of-nine Series did the money shift toward the Reds.

In contrast to Cincinnati's joy at its first championship, the atmosphere on the South Side of Chicago was grim. Jealousy and insecurity pervaded the team. Many players barely spoke to Eddie Collins, who had come over from the Philadelphia Athletics with his lofty $15,000 salary. Cliques formed. Players grumbled and threatened to quit. And at the bottom of the discontent sat the one person capable of instilling harmony and purpose: the team's owner, Charles Comiskey.

Comiskey, known as the "Old Roman" for his prominent nose, was a man who pinched a dime as hard as a bush-leaguer squeezing a train ticket from Peoria to St. Louis. Even amidst a gaggle of tightwad owners he stood out, complaining even about the expense of laundering uniforms. And his stinginess was uncalled for. The White Sox were one of the most popular teams of the era, leading the major leagues in attendance for the entire decade. The sullen players who took the field for him chafed in the awareness that they remained among the most poorly paid in the game.

The Series opened at Redland Field in Cincinnati on October 1. Though wary of the storied batsmen from the West, the crowd of nearly 31,000 arrived lighthearted, thrilled to be part of the Reds' first World Series. Appropriate to the occasion, John Philip Sousa and his marching band stirred the crowd during the pregame festivities with a rendition of his popular composition, "Stars and Stripes Forever."

The Reds began with a run in the first inning against Chicago's Eddie Cicotte. They added five more in the fourth inning and knew no danger, eventually winning 9-1. The second game was closer, but Cincinnati won again, beating Lefty Williams 4-2, and the Reds carried a 2-0 Series lead into Comiskey Park. The rivals split Games Three and Four, preparing the scene for Game Five when Hod Eller would pitch himself into the record book.

Eller's strikeout streak began in the second inning when Chick Gandil went out swinging. The next two batters, Swede Risberg and Ray Schalk, each struck out looking. In the third inning both Williams and Nemo Liebold were called out. Up next came Eddie Collins.

Collins anchored his feet in the sandy soil of the batter's box, hiked his oversize bat up a trifle higher, and scrutinized the pink-cheeked pitcher once more. He'd just witnessed ample demonstration of the effectiveness of the shine ball through the five teammates before him who stepped to the plate only to return to the dugout in humiliation. He waited the count to three balls and two strikes. A walk, he knew, would break the chain of strikeouts, perhaps motivating his listless team to overcome the scoreless tie. With the Sox down in the Series three games to one, this was a must-win contest.

Hod Eller held the ball to his chest, out of the batter's view, and worked it beneath his gaze like a shopper inspecting a fruit. When his fingers found the right grip, he rubbed the ball deliberately on his trouser leg and nodded to his catcher. Ready at last, he bowed forward slightly, then heaved back and threw.

In the instant accorded to him by his extraordinary reflexes, Eddie Collins measured the pitch and swung. But the ball dipped as if on a string, and the accelerating bat found no substance as it slashed through its arc. He was out, the sixth strikeout in a row, becoming part of Eller's World Series mark that stands today.

And October 6, 1919, was Eller's day. He finished the afternoon in a shutout, 5-0, to build his team an overmastering four-games-to-one lead in the unusual best-of-nine Series.

A brief three days later he returned to start the eighth game. And though he pitched less spectacularly, his complete-game 10-5 victory that day gave the Cincinnati Reds their first World Series championship. His two wins and his tight 2.00 earned run average conferred a fitting polish on an almost chimerical season during which he won 20 games and pitched a no-hitter.

In the style of the times, adoring fans wrote poems in praise of his strikeout feat in Game Five, the turning point of the Series. *The Sporting News* reported that Eller became "Emperor of the Series" that day. That fall the same publication praised him as one of the new heroes of the national game, a man on his way to rank beside Ty Cobb and Walter Johnson. Few fans could disagree. Hod Eller ruled the sporting world.

That world, moreover, was unaware that he had other reasons to be proud of himself. In 1976, Hod's old teammate Edd Roush repeated to sportswriter Dick Stodghill of *The Municipal Evening Press* an earlier story that Eller had been offered $5,000 by a gambler to throw the final game, but that Hod advised the would-be briber that if he ever saw him again, he'd "punch him in the nose."

If true, it is unfortunate that the story surfaced so late, for Hod enjoyed the most momentary of reigns as emperor. Within days after the Series ended, speculative news articles on the validity of the Reds victory circulated in the papers. Then, in January, came the astounding news that Babe Ruth had been sold to the New York Yankees. Thus in contrast to their customary off-season tributes to world champions, the media treated Hod Eller and the Reds with regal indifference.

Eller's strikeout record remains as obscure as the echo of the cheers that accompanied its maker. While few among the 35,000 fans in their bowlers and dark suits that afternoon in Chicago's Comiskey Park felt they could soon forget what they'd seen, they did indeed forget—as did others and then others yet, until generations later when scarcely a fan knew or cared that in his day Hod Eller was as perturbing a figure as ever seized the pitcher's mound.

That the baseball world then and now ignored the winners comes as little surprise, for the opponents of Hod Eller and his Cincinnati Reds that Series of 1919 were the Chicago White Sox, infamously known as the Black Sox for their eight players accused of throwing the Series in exchange for payments from professional gamblers. It remains a sad and impenetrable study of our society that we remember our wretches longer than our heroes.

Even before the Series ended rumors of something amiss had circulated among insiders. Normally reliable players such as Eddie Cicotte, winner of 29 games for the White Sox, became inept as he allowed six runs in less that four innings of the opening game. Ordinarily steady Swede Risberg committed four errors at shortstop. Lefty Williams won 23 games during the season, but lost all three of his Series starts.

Throughout the winter and into the next season, attention became focused on the White Sox as never before on a loser. Charges were followed by denials until ultimately Judge Landis banned forever from playing in the major leagues eight Chicago players, including the tragic Shoeless Joe Jackson, a player so brilliantly gifted that he batted over .400 his first full season in the majors.

Meanwhile, Hod Eller began the slide that would not end until six years later when he was out of baseball and forgotten. In 1920 he found his effectiveness reduced. He quarreled with Reds President August Herrmann after Herrmann suspended him for a supposed failure to get in shape. Herrmann, who has been called "the Calvin Griffith of his day," established himself as much a rival of Charles Comiskey at pinch-penny book-keeping as on the field. In one letter to Herrmann, Eller pleaded for reimbursement on train tickets from his old home town of Muncie, Indiana to Cincinnati.

Eller encountered a greater threat to his career, however, in a rule modification initiated in time for the 1920 season. Baseball changed in response to the attention the public accorded Babe Ruth. Fans became bewitched by the home run, and the new rule changes favored hitters. In late 1919, the spitball, shine ball, emery ball, and similar pitches were outlawed, save for a designated two pitchers from each team who were allowed to use the spitter for one year only.

Hod Eller continued without his shiner. In a newspaper interview he stated gamely that he had never used the shine ball "all that much." He explained that the main advantage of the pitch was to keep the hitters off balance and to "look only for shiners." His record backs him up. Though he dropped to 13 wins, his earned run average remained low while playing for a team weakened from the previous season.

Yet by 1921 Eller became the forgotten man of the sixth-place Reds' pitching staff. He finished the season with only two wins and appeared in a scant 13 games while continuing his quibbling with Herrmann over salary and training conditions. A newspaper story that season by Frederick Lieb was subheaded: "Eller's Shine Ball Talk of Country in 1919—Now 'Hod' is Bench Warmer."

Strangely, the rule makers now relented on the year-old spitball ruling. They ordered the pitch banned henceforth by all except several designated spitball pitchers who were given permission to ply the pitch for the duration of their careers. Not so the shineballers, however. Hod Eller made a personal appeal to the president of the National League, charging that he'd been denied his "stock in trade." But it brought him no satisfaction. The rule remained.

In the context of time one must wonder why the rule makers pardoned the spitter while banning other similarly behaving pitches such as the shineball. After all, the spitter had already encountered disrepute. Some believed Carl Mays killed Ray Chapman with the pitch in 1920. It is, perhaps, instructive to speculate on the association between the shineball and the Black Sox scandal.

Shineballer Eddie Cicotte, the most successful pitcher in baseball in 1919, became the first to confess his part in throwing the Series. The scandal erupted onto the incredulous public only weeks before the announcement of the rule change allowing some continued use of the spitter. Was the shineball banned because of the sudden notoriety of its best-known advocate? We can never know. But it seems possible that Hod Eller, because he used the shineball and because he pitched in that ignoble

World Series, lost his appeal for permission to resume using the pitch. And if so, Hod was twice victimized by the Black Sox.

Inevitably Cincinnati disentangled itself of Eller, probably because Herrmann regarded him a troublemaker on top of his diminished effectiveness. In 1922 the Reds traded him to Oakland of the Coast League for third baseman Babe Pinelli.

Hod clung to baseball for a couple more erratic years. After Oakland he signed on with Mobile in the Southern League. He managed Mount Sterling in the old Blue Grass League in 1923, and the following year played for Little Rock and Indianapolis before retiring in 1925. Although his career languished after 1919, his later experience cannot diminish his achievements. He never had a losing season in the majors.

With a wife and two children, an eighth-grade education, and no baseball pension awaiting him, Eller went to work as a policeman in Indianapolis. He remained one until he retired in 1947.

Years passed. In 1954 he listed himself as a candidate for Sheriff of Marion County, but managed only a few thousand votes as he finished a weak third. The days of his victories fell long in the past. On July 18, 1961, he died at age 67. He rests now beneath a plain stone in Crown Hill Cemetery in Indianapolis, not far from the graves of Benjamin Harrison, Booth Tarkington, and other Hoosier heroes.

While Hod Eller drifted into obscurity, fame and honor settled on many of his contemporaries. His former manager, Christy Mathewson, entered the Hall of Fame in 1936. Ray Schalk, one of the innocent Black Sox, was elected in 1955, and Edd Roush in 1962. Even Charles Comiskey, whose parsimony represented the seminal condition of the scandal, found distinction in Cooperstown.

Eller himself, while never disputing the evidence of the scandal, always maintained that the White Sox were "playing for keeps" that long-ago day. While three of the strikeout victims were conspirators, two of the three innocents (Schalk and Collins) reached the Hall of Fame. The MacMillan *Baseball Encyclopedia* states flatly, "there is no taint in the record."

Curiously, Hod Eller was not a man to hold a lifetime grudge against baseball. A one-page biographical form on file with the National Baseball Hall of Fame Library contains a final question that touches the heart of anyone who has ever loved the game.

"If you had to do it all over," the question states, "would you play professional baseball?"

Hod Eller, diseased with cancer and 35 years out of the game, filled out his form in 1960 at age 66. The hand that once propelled a ball so deftly had grown unsteady with age, his penmanship difficult to read.

But the handwriting becomes strong, clear, and definite when Hod responded to that final question. "Yes," he said, with perhaps the memory of that marvelous fifth game of the 1919 World Series glowing as bright as an unrubbed baseball in his heart.

RUTH'S FIRST RIVAL

Mark Alvarez

IT'S HARD IN RETROSPECT to comprehend how gigantic a phenomenon Babe Ruth was in the early 20s. He had single-handedly recreated the sport, changing it from a cagey game of speed and finesse to a display of power that dismayed and disturbed many old fans, but that thrilled the general public. He hit more home runs than entire teams, and in each of the seasons of 1919, 1920, and 1921, he more than doubled the homer totals of any other player in either league. "Sultan of Swat" was more than just a handy, alliterative nickname when it was applied to Ruth. It was an acknowledgement that he was *the* slugger—dominant, untouchable.

But in 1922, the Babe was suspended for the season's first month by Commissioner Kenesaw Mountain Landis. Ruth, who was as impressed by his Sultanship as anyone, had challenged the Judge—he'd gone barnstorming the previous fall against the Commissioner's express orders—and lost. Partisans of the new-style game were desolated. Here's how *Baseball Magazine* put it:

"Judge Landis' now famous decree struck like an early frost on the spring crop of four-base wallops. Market quotations on circuit swats sagged way under par. For what batter could hope to fill the slugger king's exalted station while the kind was temporarily bereft of his crown?"

When another player *did* step in and started hitting balls out of the park at a Ruthian rate, the baseball world was astonished.

"That seeming miracle has happened," *Baseball Magazine* breathlessly reported. Another player rose to the occasion, and did as well as Ruth had ever done in the first weeks of the season . . . Kenneth Williams was this stalwart figure who picked up the king's idle bludgeon in true kingly fashion."

Ruth returned to lead the league in slugging average, and he managed 35 homers, but Ken Williams, left fielder for the St. Louis Browns, hung onto the lead he'd built up during that month's head start, and he became the first man in the lively-ball era to take the home run crown away from the Babe. Williams had a fine career, but today it's this feat he's remembered for when he's remembered at all.

Ken Williams was born in 1890 in Grant's Pass, Oregon. He started his professional career late, and as early as 1913, his first season with Regina in the Western Canada League, he was apparently giving out his birth date as 1893. He moved on to Edmonton, then Spokane of the Northwestern League, and came to the attention of the Reds the old-fashioned way—a letter from a local businessman to Cincinnati President Gerry Herrman.

The Reds gave him a fair shot, but in 71 games with them in 1915 he hit only .242 and showed neither power nor speed. Early the next year, Cincinnati shipped him back to Spokane. He moved to Portland of the strong Pacific Coast League, and was set to report to St. Louis in 1918, but, with World War I still raging, entered the service instead.

By baseball standards, Ken Williams was an old man when he made it to the major leagues for good. When he finally got his chance with the Browns in 1919, he was almost 29—though he was still owing to three years less.

His second time around, though, Williams was the right man in the right place at the right time. He was a free-swinging "extra base slugger and timely swatter" in an era when the ball was being juiced up and men who could pound the ball were increasingly in demand. And his connection with St. Louis was a match made in baseball heaven. The Brownies, led by their great first baseman George Sisler, were entering their greatest days, and Sportsman's Park might have been built for left-handed power hitters.

Williams was built like a ballplayer. That 1922 *Baseball Magazine* article compared him to the Babe: "Save in height alone there is no physical comparison between Williams and Ruth. Babe is massive and stocky and his whole build speaks eloquently of rugged strength. Williams is tall, but rather slender. He is of the wiry type and while Babe outweighs him by at least forty pounds there is no lack of strength in Williams' long whipcord arms and his stringy, muscular legs. Williams is a rangy player, tough and seasoned . . . he stands a good six feet in his stockings and weighs 178 pounds. . . . With all due respect to Babe, Williams doesn't have to exert himself to hold up his end of the fielding game. In base running, Williams is, of course, Babe's superior."

In the same article, Williams himself may have accounted for his relative failure in the dead-ball National League of 1915 as opposed to his spectacular success in the lively-ball American of the 20s: "I was always a natural slugger. I use a heavy bat, 48 ounces. [Today's free-swingers commonly use bats that weigh 32 to 34 ounces.] I swing from the handle and grip the handle with as much strength as I have in my fingers and I swing from my toes."

After three seasons in the American League, Williams had established himself as one of the premier outfielders in baseball. In 1921 he had the first of five extraordinary years: 24 home runs (tied for second behind Ruth's 59), 117 RBI, 115 runs scored, 20 stolen bases, and a .347 batting average. The Browns, after coming in fifth and fourth in the previous two years, edged up to third, their best finish since 1902.

Nineteen-twenty-two was Williams'—and the Browns'—greatest year. The Browns peaked, losing the pennant by a single game to the Yankees after a tight race to the wire. Williams led the league in homers (39), RBI (155), and total bases (367), and was second to Sisler in stolen bases (37), third in runs (128), and second in slugging average (.627). He had 194 hits and a .332 batting average.

At one point during the season, he hit six homers in six games to set a record. At another, he hit six balls out of the park in four games to set a second. He also became the first American League player to hit three home runs in a single game. He became the first player—and the only one until Willie Mays in 1956—to hit 30 home runs and steal 30 bases in a season.

Despite his great year for a contending team, though, Williams didn't even come close to winning the Most Valuable Player Award. His teammate Sisler batted .420 and also led the league in hits, runs, triples, and stolen bases. Under the rules then in force, writers could vote for only one man per team, and the revered Sisler—in those days generally considered Cobb's successor as the game's greatest player—was everybody's St. Louis choice. He won the MVP with all but five of the possible 64 first-place votes. Over the next two years, Williams averaged .340, and, although he missed a third of the 1924 season with a broken ankle, he had 29 and 18 home runs and 91 and 84 RBI.

In the middle of the 1923 season, he ran into trouble with American League President Ban Johnson. Williams had been using a "plugged" bat, but instead of plugging his bat with cork, as is the modern players' illegal wont, or with iron as some old-timers had done, Williams apparently plugged his ash bat with a chunk of the very similar hickory. Nonetheless, Johnson told him—and Babe Ruth, who had been using a laminated bat—to cease and desist.

The Sporting News thought the whole thing was a tempest in a teapot: "The advantages of a bat with a separate piece of wood in the end appealed only to one of Ken Williams' temperament. If the genius of home runs for the Browns had been presented with a bat painted bright blue, and he had managed to get a few homers with it, he probably would just as vociferously stated bright blue bats had more hits in them than bats painted red."

This reference to Williams' temperament makes him sound like a bit of a flake. According to friends who knew him later in life, Williams did like a joke, but on the field he was, according to George Sisler, Jr., president of the American Association Columbus Clippers and the son of Williams' most famous teammate, "a quiet, unassuming man. He went about his work in a methodical way."

In 1925, Williams was methodically thumping his way to what he later said "would have been my best season" when, on August 14, he was beaned by Indian submariner Byron Speece. Williams spent ten days in the hospital and was then sent home, his season over. He'd accumulated 25 home runs, 105 RBI and a batting average of .331. His slugging average of .613 led the league.

Over the winter, Williams experienced headaches and dizzy spells, and they persisted into spring training. Late in the 1926 season, *Baseball Magazine*, in remembering the beaning, claimed that Williams "has what seems to be unavoidable in such cases, a tendency to back away from the ball."

Whether it was recurring dizziness, an inability to hang in there against left handers, or simply his age catching up with him, Williams was never again quite the same player. He had 17 home runs and 74 RBI in both 1926 and 1927, then was sold to the Boston Red Sox in a St. Louis house cleaning that also saw Sisler move to Washington. Williams played out the string in Boston for two more mediocre seasons. In 1930, the Yankees bought him—ironically—as insurance during a Babe Ruth holdout. When Ruth returned, Williams was released before the season started. His major-league baseball career was over.

Back home in Grant's Pass, Williams became a policeman, and later bought a bar and billiard room. Old-timers remember him helping out with the high school team and the semi-pro Grant's Pass Merchants. Harlan James, a retired pressman at the Grant's Pass *Courier* also remembers him as "a crackerjack billiard player—better than anybody in this part of the country."

Ken Williams hung up some great numbers during his career—especially over that five-season stretch from 1921 throught 1925. Comparing his production during those years with that of contemporary outfielders like Ruth, Bob and Irish Meusel, George Kelly, Cy Williams, Harry Heilman, Tris Speaker and Ty Cobb, it's clear that he was at the top of his profession.

Bill Borst, the enthusiastic founder and president of the St. Louis Browns Historical Society, calls Williams "the most underrated Brownie," and is pushing for his admission to the Baseball Hall of Fame. George Sisler, Jr. says, "He was a great hitter and a fine outfielder. He should be at least considered for the Hall of Fame." Others who look at the record agree.

But there is another county to be heard from. In his *Historical Abstract*, Bill James calls Williams "an interesting player," but says "his credentials to be called a great one are shaky at best." Statistician Pete Palmer has demonstrated that Williams was one of the greatest home-park hitters in the history of baseball. "He hit 72% of his homers at home," says Palmer. "Of players with a hundred or more home runs, that's the highest percentage all-time." In 1922, 32 of Williams' 39 homers were hit in Sportsman's Park. Over his career with the Browns, according to Palmer, Williams hit .341, with a .632 slugging average at home, .310, with a .480 SA on the road.

Others simply argue that a terrific five years in a longer, solid career isn't enough to qualify a player for the Hall.

The facts are interesting, but the argument is boring. Election to the Hall—especially for old-timers—has come to be so tenuously related to the actual value of a player in his heyday that it says relatively little about a player's true worth on the field.

But before he died of heart failure in January of 1959, Ken Williams did receive an honor that meant a lot to him. In 1958, he was chosen a member of the all-time St. Louis team by local baseball writers. He traveled to St. Louis for the banquet, and Bob Broeg remembered the event this way in a 1974 column in *The Sporting News:* "Ken Williams was amiable, almost blase, until he was handed a plaque that listed him in a lineup that included George Sisler, Rogers Hornsby, Frank Frisch and Stan Musial, among others.

"Then the composure left. . . . He broke down, explaining as he held the plaque aloft:

"'Now, with this, maybe I can convince the kids around the bar back home in Oregon . . . that I was almost as good as I said I was.'"

SANDLOT BABE

Edward "Dutch" Doyle

ON SEPTEMBER 4, 1923, Babe Ruth, playing in Philadelphia, pulled a Granspach pitch deep over the right field fence. Observers say that the ball may have traveled as far as 600 feet. Instead of a colossal home run, though, Ruth was credited with what may be the longest two-base hit in baseball history.

You see, he wasn't playing for the Yankees in Shibe Park, but for Ascension Catholic in their sandlot enclosure on the corner of 1st and Tioga, where any ball hit over the short right field fence was a ground rule double.

At the time, the Yanks were driving down the stretch to their third straight pennant and the Babe had a battle of his own going with Harry Heilman for the batting championship. Whatever possessed Babe Ruth to get involved in a sandlot game in the Kensington section of Philadelphia?

The reason was Ascension's Father Casey. The good Father, a great baseball fan and the unofficial chaplain of Connie Mack's Philadelphia Athletics, had built the enclosure hoping to make money for the church by holding ball games there. It was an excellent facility for Philadelphia's thriving independent baseball clubs, but Father Casey had gone deeply into debt to build it. Now, the construction had to be paid off.

Taking the direct approach, Father Casey asked his friend Babe Ruth if he would play with Ascension against Lit Brothers. The Ascension Club was by no means just a church baseball team. It was an excellent semi-pro team sponsored by a Philadelphia department store. Father knew that the Babe would pull in a huge crowd, and he hoped that he might be able to pay off the enclosure in a single shot.

The Babe said yes. Why? Probably, mostly because, as Red Smith wrote in *Strawberries in Summertime*, "The man was a boy, simple, artless, genuine, unabashed." He'd been asked to help out a friend—and a priest to boot. Of course he said yes.

There was just one hitch: the Babe had a little other business to transact that day. The Yankees were scheduled to play the Athletics at 3:15.

Now the enclosure at 1st and Tioga had no lights, of course, so Father Casey scheduled the Ascension-Lit Brothers game for twilight, organized things as best he could, and prayed for the best. He had an Ascension uniform specially made for the Babe. He had a taxi standing by at Shibe Park. And he needed a quick game. Father Casey had extreme faith in the heavens, and the Yankees had Sam Jones.

Jones was all that was needed that day. He no-hit the A's in one hour and twenty-three minutes.

Moments later, the Babe was practically flying toward Kensington. There are several versions of where Babe actually changed into his Ascension uniform. Some people say that he put it on at Shibe. Others remember that Father Casey brought him right to the rectory in his Yankee uniform and he changed there. Either way, by the time he arrived at the enclosure, the whole neighborhood was seething with fans who wanted to see him. According to the Philadelphia *Inquirer*, "The largest crowd that ever saw an independent game in Philadelphia was on hand. Every seat was taken in the grandstand and hundreds stood both in the field and inside the enclosure. Up the hill alongside of the Pennsylvania Railroad tracks were several thousands more, while mill windows and housetops held their quota also." The crowd was estimated at 10,000—twice as many spectators as had seen Jones's no-hitter at Shibe Park earlier in the day.

Fans who saw the Yankees a lot in those days knew that the Babe loved to play first base. Every day after the infield regulars were finished, he'd go and play first and put on a show. Not surprisingly, then, he chose to play first base for Ascension. This may have been a minor disappointment to those who had hoped to see him pitch, but nobody left.

When the Babe first came up, the umpire stopped the game and the players led by Father Casey walked toward home plate and presented him with a diamond stick pin.

This astounded even Babe Ruth, who gracefully accepted, claiming, according to the *Inquirer*, "that he could not express how much the gift meant."

As the game proceeded, he gave the crowd its money's worth. Early on, he ripped his uniform diving after a vicious line drive, and he continued to play as if the World Series were on the line.

He was playing so hard that Billy Ferguson, the Ascension manager and the long-time basketball coach at St. Joseph's University, began to worry. "Here was Babe Ruth in our neighborhood, playing with our church team and the Yankees were in first place and Ruth was batting .390 and battling Harry Heilman for the batting title," he said later. All Ferguson could think of were headlines in every paper in the country: "Babe Breaks Leg In Sandlot Game."

Ruth himself obviously didn't share these concerns. The only things on his mind seemed to be giving the fans a treat and winning the ball game.

In the eighth inning the Babe went out to left field with a bucket of balls and tossed them into the stands and over the fence to the thousands of youngsters who couldn't get in. In the ninth, he brought out a fungo bat and hit ball after ball out to a wild scramble of kids.

At first base, the Babe was flawless, with 13 putouts and two assists. His gargantuan double in his second at bat was his only hit of the game, but not his only offensive contribution. In the bottom of the ninth, with Ascension down 2-0, he hit a towering fly to left center field, which Marshall misplayed for a two-base error. Catcher Charley White walked and Babe sensed an opportunity to tie the score. Ruth in those days carried 205 or 210 pounds on his 6′2″ frame. And he was fast—he stole home ten times in his major-league career. Now he flashed the steal sign to White.

Barger, the Lit Brothers catcher, fired to second to get White, but the Babe, with his splendid peripheral vision, did not break stride as he rounded third and roared into home with a great slide to score Ascension's only run. Lit Brothers prevailed, 2-1.

After the game, Babe remained at home plate well into the night giving autographs to every kid who wanted one. During the game, he had signed several dozen balls for Father Casey who later sold them as five-dollar souvenirs—a big money-maker.

There's no record of how much money the Babe brought in for his friend Father Casey, but there's little doubt that he paid off the enclosure at 1st and Tioga. Teams played there up until World War II or so. But there was certainly never another game like the one in which Babe Ruth played for Ascension Catholic.

THE 26-INNING DUEL

Norman L. Macht

ON MAY 1, 1920, Joe Oeschger looked up from the newspaper and laughed. "The weather forecast says fair today," the 6'1", 195-pound Boston Braves pitcher said to his roommate, outfielder Les Mann. They both glanced out the window. It was raining steadily, a cold, grey, wet and windy morning, not unusual for the first day of May in Boston.

They went down to the dining room of the Brunswick Hotel, where they shared a room when the team was home, ordered breakfast and divided the newspaper.

They read the *Globe's* account of the Friday game. Braves teammate Hugh McQuillan had shut out the Brooklyn Dodgers, 3 to 0. The game had taken just over an hour and a half.

"Who's playing for the Dodgers today, if we play?" Mann asked.

"It looks like Cadore. Golly," Oeschger said, "I'd like to get even with him." Ten days before the two had hooked up in an 11-inning duel, Dodger's Cadore winning it, 1 to 0.

"Maybe next time we go to Brooklyn."

There was no mention of the Boston probable pitcher. Braves Manager George Stallings liked to wait until just before game time to name his starter.

Oeschger, the pitcher, checked the standings. Brooklyn, their scheduled opponent, was 8 and 4, in second place. They were fast, had some good hitters led by Zack Wheat, and had a top-flight pitching staff. They had won the pennant in 1916 and, some predicted, would make it tough for the favored Giants in 1920.

The Braves were 4 and 5. They had gotten great pitching so far, were strong defensively, but were weak at the plate; nobody was hitting over

.250. Since their 1914 come-from-behind pennant victory and four-game upset of the Philadelphia Athletics in the World Series, they had gradually slid into the second division.

"Looks like a weekend off," Mann said. "What do you want to do?"

"Guess we'll go to a show."

They finished a leisurely breakfast at noon and went out on the porch overlooking the Back Bay section of the city. The rain had stopped. The cold wind had not. Manager Stallings had a standing rule: all players had to report to the clubhouse even if it was pouring. So Oeschger and Mann went up to their room for some sweaters, then walked up Commonwealth Avenue to Braves Field.

Oeschger watched the trainer, Jimmy Neery, put a clean bandage on shortstop Rabbit Maranville's left hand. The Rabbit had been playing outstanding games in the field with a bruised, lacerated hand for the past few days. He'd had a few shots of whiskey already—it was never too early in the day for Rabbit to down a few. Then Oeschger had a rubdown.

At 2:30 there was a brief, heavy shower but the clouds scudded quickly out to sea. About 3,500 hardy fans had bundled up and sat, huddled in pockets scattered about the 38,000-seat stands. Just 15 minutes before the 3:00 o'clock game time, they decided to play the game. It was just one ball game—one Saturday afternoon's action on the diamond—but it would put two sub-.500 pitchers into the record books forever.

Stallings was very superstitious and given to playing hunches. Bats had to be placed in exact order and kept that way, especially during a rally. The drinking cup had to hang just so on the water cooler spigot. A southern gentleman who had gone to Johns Hopkins intending to become a doctor, Stallings seldom wore a uniform. He stayed in the dugout, impeccably dressed in street clothes.

Stallings posted the day's lineup in the dugout. On the road he pitched Oeschger—a regular churchgoer—on Sundays, probably figuring he'd have the Lord on his side. But strangely enough, Stallings would start Oeschger today, Saturday.

Over in the visitors clubhouse, Wilbert Robinson was entertaining the writers with stories of the good old days. A kindhearted, affable, rotund fellow, Uncle Robbie was a veteran of the old Baltimore Orioles, a teammate of McGraw, whom he replaced as manager of the Orioles when McGraw took over the New York Giants in the middle of the 1902 season.

He finished his career in 1931 with two pennant winners in his 19 years at Brooklyn, spent most of his time in the second division, but was very popular.

Robbie wasn't much for pre-game meetings, but Stallings held a skull session before every game. He went over the Dodger batting order:

Ivy Olson—second base, strictly a pull hitter;

Bernie Neis—right field, good fastball hitter and base stealer;

Jimmy Johnston—third base, fastball hitter and base stealer;

Zack Wheat—left field, exceptionally good hitter with tendency to pull to right field;

Hy Myers—center field, fast and a good bunter;

Ed Konetchy—first base, hits to all fields, slow runner;

Chuck Ward—shortstop, hits to all fields, not a long ball threat;

Ernie Krueger—catcher, good pull hitter, play shortstop and third baseman toward the line.

While the pitchers were warming up, one of the Brooklyn players casually wandered in front of the home team dugout and scattered some peanuts. A few damp pigeons swooped down.

"Get those birds out of here," Stallings said. He hated pigeons, and the other teams knew it. He wore out his benchwarmers' arms throwing pebbles to chase the birds.

Both pitchers were in top condition. Built alike they had been the most effective hurlers in the early going.

Boston's Oeschger had given up two earned runs in 35 innings. He was a fastball pitcher.

Brooklyn's Cadore had pitched 35 scoreless innings against the Yankees on the trip north from spring training. He had shut out Boston in that 11-inning game April 20, but had lost his last start against the Giants. He was a curveball specialist.

The umpires were William McCormick, a second-year man, behind the plate, and Robert F. Hart, a rookie, on the bases.

The temperature was 49 when Oeschger threw the first pitch.

They ran off four fast, scoreless innings.

In the top of the fifth, Oeschger dug a hole for himself. He pitched too carefully to Krueger, the pull hitter, and walked him. Cadore then hit a sharp bounder to the mound, a perfect double-play ball. In his anxiety to get two, Oeschger juggled the ball and lost the chance. He threw out

Cadore at first. With a two-strike count, Olson hit a broken-bat blooper over Maranville's head that scored Krueger.

When the inning ended, Oeschger stalked off the mound muttering to himself for his clumsiness.

As if to make up for his misplay, he led off the bottom of the fifth with a long double, but was left stranded at second.

Outfielder Wally Cruise, first up in the last of the sixth, hit a line-drive triple off the scoreboard in left. Walt Holke then blooped a Texas leaguer back of shortstop. Zack Wheat raced in and took it off his shoetops just behind the infield dirt. Cruise was halfway home; he thought it might drop in. The third baseman had gone out after the ball, so there was nobody on third to take a throw from Wheat and Cruise was spared. Tony Boeckel followed with a single to center, scoring Cruise with the tying run.

Maranville laced a double to right center. Wally Hood chased it down and threw home as Boeckel rounded third. Cadore cut off the throw and relayed it home in time to nip Boeckel. The Brooklyn catcher, Krueger, was spiked on the play and was replaced by Rowdy Elliott.

Joe Oeschger went out for the seventh inning even more angry at himself. But for his poor fielding in the fifth, he would have a 1-0 lead now, and the way he was going he was confident that would have been enough. He bore down and retired the side on three pitches.

They went down to the ninth. Cadore had been hit harder, but was saved by several fielding gems. In the eighth, Mann led off with a single. Walt Cruise sacrificed him to second. Holke lined one back through the box which Cadore instinctively batted down and threw him out, saving the winning run. Twice more he stopped line drives that would have scored a run. Wheat and Neis were pulling off impossible catches.

The Braves, too, were on fire in the field. Catcher Mickey O'Neil picked off two runners at first base.

Boston looked like they would win it in the ninth. Maranville led off with a base hit to left. Lloyd Christenbury pinch hit for O'Neil and bunted down the first base line. Cadore fielded it, but the throw hit the runner in the back as he stepped on the base. Oeschger sacrificed them to second and third. Ray Powell walked. With the bases full and one out, the Brooklyn infield played in. Charlie Pick hit a sharp hopper toward right. Second baseman Ivy Olson stabbed it, swiped at Powell coming down from first and threw to first for the double play. Powell had gone out of the baseline to avoid the tag and was called out.

So they went into the 10th, the 11th, the 12th, the 13th, the 14th. Three up, three down for the Dodgers, little more for the Braves.

Hank Gowdy, another hero of the 1914 triumph, replaced O'Neil behind the plate in the 10th inning. He had trouble holding onto Oeschger's pitches, boxing the ball, dropping it more often than catching it.

Gowdy went to the mound.

"What the hell are you throwing?" he asked.

"Just a fastball."

"God Almighty, it's breaking one way one time and somewhere else the next time."

"Well," Oeschger replied, "I don't know which way it's going to move either."

It began to drizzle in the 11th. The wind blew in from center field. It was getting colder. Necks, backs and arms were chilled by the cold and dampness; muscles tightened. Between innings, players on both sides put on heavy sweaters.

The Braves threatened in the 15th. Cruise walked. Holke hit a little dribbler toward third. Johnston tried to make a play at second but was too late. Two on, nobody out. Boeckel put down a bunt but the ball stopped dead on the soggy third-base line and Elliott picked it up and forced Cruise at third. Maranville grounded back to Cadore and Holke was forced at third. Gowdy flied out.

Oeschger led off the 16th determined to win his own game. He hit a shot that looked like it might clear the left field scoreboard. Wheat, using the fence for a springboard, jumped up and caught it. Oeschger scuffed the dirt by second base as he headed back to the dugout. That would have been the ball game.

As they took the field for the 17th, Rabbit Maranville chirped, "Just one more inning, Joe. We'll get a run for you. Hold on."

The Rabbit kept up a steady stream of chatter and encouragement on the field.

Oeschger was beginning to tire. Still, he thought, if Stallings asks if I want to come out, my answer will be an emphatic no.

Stallings never asked. "Hold them one more inning, Joe," was all he said. "We'll get them."

The Dodgers came this close to winning it in the 17th. Zack Wheat opened with a single to right. Hood sacrificed him to second. Konetchy grounded sharply to Maranville who couldn't handle it. Base hit. First and third. One out. Chuck Ward bounced to Maranville who threw to third hoping to catch Wheat off the base. But Zack was wary and scrambled back ahead of the throw. Bases loaded. One out.

Rowdy Elliott was up. The catcher hit back to the mound. This time Oeschger fielded it cleanly and threw home to force Wheat. Gowdy's throw to first was over Elliott's head and to the right of the base. Holke dove to his left and knocked the ball down as Elliott crossed the bag. Konetchy rounded third and bolted for home. The left handed first baseman threw home while going down. The throw was on the first-base side of the plate. Gowdy reached out and caught it and lunged through the air across home plate, the ball in his bare hand, into the spikes of Konetchy sliding in. Koney bumped the ball with his shin, but Gowdy held on and the threat was over. It was the last one for the Robins.

Ordinarily fans like to see plenty of hits and scoring. They were getting more than their money's worth of pitching and fielding thrills. Despite the uncomfortable weather, nobody left the park. After the 18th inning they cheered each pitcher as he left the mound or came up to bat.

In the Dodgers dugout, veteran pitcher Rube Marquard, who had pitched plenty of long games himself, said to Cadore's roommate, utility infielder Ray Schmandt, "I hope Leon won't be affected by this strain. I hate to see him stay in this long."

"Caddy is pure grit," Schmandt said. "He'll win out."

Uncle Robbie didn't have the heart to take him out. And Cadore wouldn't have come out if he were asked.

Cadore had been hit hard and often, and had at least one runner on in each of the first nine innings. But now he was aided by the enclosing twilight and the soiled, discolored ball that remained in play.

Oeschger had allowed nine hits, all singles; he gave up more than two in only one inning, the 17th. He was tired, but he had been more fatigued in some nine-inning games where he was in a lot of jams. This was an easy outing. He seemed to grow stronger as the game went on. He figured he had the advantage in the gathering dusk and did not want the game to be called. He was a fastball pitcher; Cadore, a curveballer. The hitters would have more trouble seeing his stuff. He saved himself by bearing down only when he had to, which wasn't often. The Dodgers went out in order in 18 innings.

Neither pitcher was looking for strikeouts, which take a lot of pitches. And their control was good. Oeschger wound up walking three, striking out four. Cadore walked five, struck out eight.

They wasted little time or motion. They routinely took only three or four warm-up pitches at the start of an inning, and continued to do so throughout the game. Every inning might be the last, would probably be the last, they thought.

The feeling grew on both benches that it would be a shame for either pitcher to lose such a game. Even the home plate umpire, McCormick, later admitted that after the 22nd inning he hoped the game would end in a tie.

The fielders never flagged. Holke took away extra base hits by snaring foul-line-hugging smashes in the 21st and 24th.

After the 17th Oeschger pitched a nine-inning no-hitter, giving up a walk in the 22nd.

At the start of the 26th, somebody in the Braves dugout wondered how long Oeschger could pitch. "He could pitch 126 innings without running any risk," said Dick Rudolph, the pitching hero of the 1914 sweep of the A's. "He's in great shape."

In the last of the 26th, with two men out, Holke beat out a bunt but Boeckel flied out.

It was 6:50 by the clock atop the scoreboard as the Dodgers came off the field. Umpire McCormick took off his mask, stepped in front of home plate and looked up at the sky. It still looked light enough to play, but for how long? Another whole inning?

Cadore watched the umpire out of the corner of his eye while walking toward the dugout.

Ivy Olson ran toward the umpire, one finger high in the air.

"One more. One more." His shrill voice carried all the way to the press box above the grandstand. Olson wanted to be able to say he had played the equal of three nine-inning games in one afternoon.

Both pitchers were willing—and able—to go one more inning.

But McCormick said no. The game was over. The fans booed.

The other players had had enough. Zack Wheat said, "I carried up enough lumber to the plate to build a house today." Charlie Pick's batting average had suffered the most—he went 0 for 11.

The darkness descended quickly at that point. Up in the press box there were no electric lights. They knew they were in for hours of work.

In addition to the Boston writers, only Eddie Murphy of the *New York Sun* and Tommy Rice of the *Brooklyn Eagle* covered the game. As the innings rolled by and other New York newspapers heard about it, the two writers were deluged with orders for special reports and stories. Somebody went out and bought a couple dozen candles, and the official scorer, the writers, and the Western Union telegraphers worked into the night by candlelight.

Cadore had pitched to 95 batters, an average of fewer than four an inning. Oeschger faced 90.

Cadore had 13 assists, a one-game record for a pitcher. Oeschger had 11.

Oeschger had set a record for consecutive scoreless innings in one game: 21. Cadore had 20.

First baseman Walter Holke had 32 put-outs and one assist.

Only three Dodgers had reached third: Krueger, who scored, and Wheat and Konetchy, who were erased in the double play in the 17th.

They didn't count pitches in those days. Cadore later estimated he had thrown close to 300; Oeschger guessed about 250.

Game time was 3 hours and 50 minutes.

James C. O'Leary typed out his lead for the *Boston Globe:*

"It was one of the greatest games ever played, but on account of the threatening weather only about 4,000 turned out. They stayed til the end. And saw the most wonderful pitching stunt ever performed, and some classy playing and thrilling situations. It was a battle of giants until both were exhausted practically, but neither gave a sign of letting up. There was glory enough for both and it would have been a pity for either one to have been declared the loser."

That evening Oeschger and Les Mann went to a restaurant they frequented. Nothing posh, just a neighborhood place with good food. It was later than usual, and the staff had heard about the game. The waitresses brought out a special cake they had made for the occasion.

The Robins had to hurry back to Brooklyn for a Sunday game against the Phillies. They were due back on Monday. Cadore stayed in Boston, with Ray Schmandt, Sherry Smith, and Rube Marquard.

Sunday morning each pitcher received a telegram from National League president John A. Heydler. He congratulated them, and said he was particularly gratified because the pitching was done under the new rules; this was the first year the spitball, emery ball, shine ball and other trick pitches were banned.

The Sunday Boston papers filled their front pages with big headlines, photos and box scores of the game. It was the talk of the the city, and the baseball world.

It has been written than when the Dodgers returned from Brooklyn on Monday, Cadore was still in bed, since Saturday night. But in fact he had kept pretty much to his hotel until Sunday afternoon, when he and his teammates went downtown to dinner, then to a picture show.

"I was a bit tired," Cadore said later, "and naturally my arm stiffened. I couldn't raise it to comb my hair for three days. After seven days of rest I was back taking my regular turn. I never had a sore arm before or after the game. I suppose the nervous energy of trying to win had given me strength and kept me going."

When Oeschger awoke Sunday morning, he was lame all over. His arm ached no more than his other limbs. His leg and back muscles had worked as hard as the arm ligaments. There was a little more soreness around his elbow.

Oeschger stayed in the Brunswick Hotel all day. He knew the cold damp winds would do more injury to him than twice the innings he had worked Saturday.

There was much speculation at the time as to what effect the long game would have on the two pitchers. Rube Marquard said, "I've been lucky. I've been in a lot of overtime games without being much affected. But the physical and mental makeup of pitchers is not all the same. I pitched a 21-inning game against Babe Adams in 1914. It didn't bother me. Three days later I shut out the Reds. But Adams was out of the big leagues the next year. He went to the American Association where he got his arm back, then came back with the Pirates and pitched until he was 43.

"It would be good judgment," concluded Marquard, "to have both men sit on the bench for at least 10 days. They should work out a bit but not get into a game before then."

Cadore felt he never had the same stuff again. He finished that year with a 15-14 record, then won 13, 8 and 4. At 33, he was finished.

It has also been written that Oeschger, too, was never the same. (On the radio following the Mets-Giants seven-hour marathon in 1964, it was mentioned that Oeschger was never worth a hill of beans as a pitcher after his long effort.)

"The 20-inning game with Brooklyn last year may have hurt my arm," he said the next day, "because I was not in the best of condition. I had passed the winter in the East and had not been able to enjoy hunting and fishing and working on my dad's ranch in California. But I'm in good condition this spring and do not expect any ill effects from yesterday's game."

Oeschger won 15 games that year, and had his best season in 1921, winning 20 and losing 14 with a second division team. He pitched 299 innings each year. He fell off to 6-21 and 5-15 the next two years, was traded back to the Giants, then the Phillies, and ended his career with a 1-2 record in—of all places—Brooklyn.

Both pitchers were remembered for that one afternoon's work for the rest of their lives. Ironically, but for his own fielding error, Joe Oeschger would have gone home happy with a nine-inning 1 to 0 victory and never been heard of again when his playing days were over. But for the next 66 years he continued to receive requests for autographs and interviews from all over the world. He had a box score of the game reprinted and would sign them and send them out.

Cadore, too, experienced his fame in unusual ways.

"I'm in a San Francisco bar one day in 1931," he recalled, "and the guy next to me is chewing the fat with his pal about extra inning ball games.

"'Yeah,' says the guy. 'Once a bum in Brooklyn pitched 26 innings. Cuddle or Coodoo or something like that.'

"'You're nuts,' says his pal. 'Nobody could pitch that long.'

"I nudged the guy sitting next to me. 'You mean Cadore?' I said.

"'Yeah, that was the bum. Cadore.'

"I took out my lifetime pass and let him look at it. 'I'm Cadore. I pitched that game.' He almost toppled off his stool."

When Cadore was in the hospital in 1958, the doctor told him they couldn't locate a vein. "A man your age should have a vein sticking right out, especially in that right arm that pitched those 26 innings."

"Doc," said Cadore, grinning, "I pitched that game with my head."

THE MAGNIFICENT PITTSBURGH CRAWFORDS

James Bankes

A SHORT, STOCKY freewheeler with an ever-present Havana cigar, William A. "Gus" Greenlee came to Pittsburgh in 1920 from Marion, North Carolina. He would become the numbers king of the city's black community; he would purchase a club on Wylie Avenue to serve as headquarters for his runners. Greenlee's Crawford Grille held sway as the most reknowned "black and tan" in the area. A sprawling two-story restaurant and dance hall, The Grille served perhaps the best food in the city.

In Greenlee's numbers game, or "the policy wheel," a gambler picked any three-digit number, and if the number turned out to be the last three digits of the race track handle, or the last three digits of the volume of the stock market, or any other predetermined number, the Greenlee organization paid off, usually at odds of 600 to 1. By betting as little as a penny, a man could win six dollars—big money, especially after the great depression rolled over America.

Greenlee established absolute mastery over Pittsburgh's North Side numbers when he was the only "honest" numbers banker who paid off after a very large hit during the late 1920's. As his wealth and power grew, Gus surrounded himself with a street-wise organization kingpinned by the sophisticated Teddy Horne, Lena Horne's father. Teddy supervised the numbers racket as well as the thriving liquor business. From time to time, ex-heavyweight boxing champion Jack Johnson also enjoyed some of the liquor action. Without stigma, Greenlee enjoyed both respect and a flashy lifestyle—the best food, the liveliest entertainment, the most expensive clothes, and a new Lincoln convertible every year. Still, the community expected support from men with money. For numbers king Gus Greenlee, this meant supporting the best black baseball team in town.

In 1930, Big Gus began to bankroll one of Pittsburgh's very best semi-pro black clubs: the Crawford Colored Giants. These Crawfords seemed a natural choice for Greenlee, as they were sponsored by the Crawford Recreation Center located at the corner of Wylie and Crawford Avenues in the heart of Pittsburgh's Hill District. Crawford Avenue served as the main drag of black Pittsburgh and the site of his own establishment.

Cumberland Willis Posey, the resourceful owner/manager of the Homestead Grays across town, was too busy to notice Greenlee's thunder. Cum joined the Grays as a player in 1911, became captain two years later, and rose to his position of power by transforming the Grays into a Pittsburgh institution, successful both on the field and at the box office. In 1930, he was putting together a powerhouse club centered around volatile first baseman Oscar Charleston, perhaps baseball's best player, Smokey Joe Williams, considered by many to be the premier pitcher in black baseball history; and the brainy clutch hitter, third baseman Judy Johnson.

Greenlee dreamed of turning the Crawfords into a black baseball dynasty, and, in 1931, he began flexing his substantial bankroll to make it happen. Realizing the need for a ballpark closer to the black community, he began construction of a new stadium complex on Bedford Avenue.

Completed during the late winter of 1932, Greenlee Field cost the numbers king a cool $100,000. Beautiful, with a seating capacity of 7,000, the park sported a playing surface as lush and spacious as any major-league field. Most significant, the complex included superb locker room facilities for both home and visiting clubs. No longer did his black players have to dress and shower in the dingy atmosphere of the Pittsburgh YMCA because the white managers of Ammon Field or Forbes Field refused them.

As his first personnel acquisition, Greenlee hired John Clark as team secretary and publicist. With this ingenious move, Greenlee converted a stinging adversary into a valuable employee. Clark had authored several blistering articles for the *Pittsburgh American* denouncing the numbers racket. Now Greenlee owned Clark's powerful pen.

Greenlee obtained the first of his franchise players late in 1931. For a mere $250, he purchased the contract of Leroy "Satchel" Paige from the disbanding Cleveland Cubs. Born in Mobile, Paige earned the nickname "Satchel" as a seven-year-old working after school as a suitcase porter at the local railroad station. By the summer of 1931, he neared dominance among black pitchers, his exquisite control and the enormous velocity of his humming bee ball overpowering most of the opposition.

By 1932, Greenlee opened his bank account for the cream of the Homestead Grays. Lured by more money and a chance to play for the organization that promised to be the classiest in all of black baseball, the brilliant veteran Oscar Charleston joined the Crawfords as playing manager. Third baseman Judy Johnson joined him as did catcher Josh Gibson, the murderous young slugger who had slammed 75 homers for the Grays in 1931.

During the 1932 season, the Crawfords combed the country challenging all comers, both black and white. They crushed most of their opposition, winning 100 while losing only 37. Much to Cum Posey's delight, and despite the serious depletion of his team's talent, the Homestead Grays beat Greenlee's Crawfords 10 out of 19 times during the year.

To establish the Crawfords as a true dynasty, Greenlee needed a dominant center fielder. By 1933, he secured the services of Cool Papa Bell, the most famous flyhawk in black baseball, a man whose flying feet sparked offensive and defensive brilliance. Bell became available when depression economics spelled doom for the St. Louis Stars. With this acquisition, the Crawfords stood on the threshold of their golden era; Greenlee, on the edge of his dream.

The original Negro National League died after the 1931 season, driven to the grave by the depression and by Rube Foster's death the previous year. Hoping to improve his finances and further solidify his legitimacy in the eyes of the common people, Greenlee led the restoration of the league prior to the 1933 season. The new NNL needed a substantial infusion of money, and Big Gus knew just the source.

Under Greenlee's leadership, the Negro National League became a stronghold of the wealthiest and most powerful black gangsters in the East. Eager to launder racket money, Ed "Soldier Boy" Semler financed the New York Black Yankees; Ed Bolden, the Philadelphia Stars; Tom Wilson, the Baltimore Elite Giants; Abe and Effa Manley, the Newark Eagles; and Alex Pompez, the New York Cubans. Even the righteous Cum Posey found himself in need of gangster money, his support coming from Rufus Jackson who ran the notorious "Night Roll" in Homestead, mastermind of the early jukebox action up and down the Monongahela. The most awesome power rested in the hands of Alex Pompez, owner of the New York Cubans and proprietor of Dyckman's Oval, Harlem's lively baseball and amusement park. Born in Key West, Pompez moved to New York City in the 1920's and became a prominent numbers specialist in the Dutch Schultz mob. By the thirties he stood as one of the richest men in Harlem.

Still, Greenlee exercised ample power himself. The Crawfords, one of the major extensions of his influence, provided him with great satisfaction. Gus wanted the best and the team became synonymous with the best in baseball, black or white. Their dream lineup of talented, confident men flashed with pride and bowed to no baseball team on earth.

Paige, the obvious leader of the pitching staff, proved to be one of Greenlee's best investments. Independent and unpredictable, yet superbly talented, Paige became the biggest drawing card in black baseball, and with the decline of Babe Ruth, perhaps in all of baseball.

Hall-of-Fame first baseman Buck Leonard knew Paige well: "Satch had great speed, but I think control was even more important to his success. He could throw the ball right at your knees all day long. It seemed to come right out of that big foot he'd stick in your face. I remember him practicing by throwing balls over matchbook covers and gum wrappers from the mound. He wasn't just lobbing the ball either. He was smoking."

Once a great outfielder, with extraordinary speed and a deadly arm, the aging Oscar Charleston danced a stylish first base for the Crawfords. Absolutely no man inspired more fear with runners in scoring position. When he fixed the pitcher with his smoldering eyes and unleashed his picture-book swing, it became obvious his skill and power as a hitter remained undiminished.

A youngster once asked Josh Gibson, the Crawfords' powerful catcher, for one of his broken bats. "Son," replied Gibson, "I don't break bats, I wear them out." Indeed, his hammer blistered screaming line drives all over the field and often beyond.

"He was without a doubt the best hitter I ever saw," says Hall-of-Famer Judy Johnson. "He hit for both consistency and power—enormous power. He had a short compact swing and never seemed to be fooled or off-balance. If he could have played in the big leagues, I think he'd hold all the power records. I'll tell you this, his bat would make him the catcher of choice for any baseball team in history."

Judy Johnson played the hot corner. A quiet, elegant man, he approached the game in an intellectual fashion and backed it up with excellent athletic ability. A clutch hitter and a brilliant defensive operative, Johnson commanded universal respect.

Centerfield belonged to Cool Papa Bell. Flying feet wove his magic.

The fastest man in baseball history, Bell delighted his many admirers by blurring on the basepaths and in the garden.

Greenlee supplemented the heart of his lineup with excellent ballplayers. Among these, Bell's two outfield flankers, speedsters Ted Page and Jimmie Crutchfield, and Alex "Double Duty" Radcliffe, so named because he once pitched the first game of a doubleheader, then caught the second.

Pleased with his club, Greenlee worked hard to keep the players happy. Ted Page recalled Greenlee's generosity: "Gus was really a great guy and he truly loved baseball. He often traveled with the team and sometimes even drove the bus himself. Greenlee was a big man in more ways than one. One winter, I didn't have a baseball job and he gave me a job in the numbers business. They had an old vacant house in Hazelwood. On the second floor, they had a long row of tables where they turned in all the numbers each day. Gus just gave me a chair and told me to sit downstairs on the sidewalk and ring a bell if anybody showed up who wasn't supposed to be there. I would just push a button and alert them upstairs to get rid of the money. That's all I did. I got paid $15 a week. I just sat in the chair every afternoon for about three hours until they finished counting the money and put it in the bank. In fact, I never had to push the button. I did practically nothing all winter for $15 a week. It was Greenlee's way of taking care of me."

During 1933, and for the next three seasons, Greenlee's dashing Crawfords dominated black baseball. While the intense rivalry between the Crawfords and the Grays proved lucrative for both Greenlee and Posey, the countryside earned more black ink than the sepia metropolis.

Greenlee promoted the first black All-Star game in Chicago during the summer of 1933. For both the entertainers and the black community, the East-West Classic highlighted the baseball summer. He hired Abe Saperstein of Harlem Globetrotter fame to handle the publicity. Despite Saperstein's efforts, the white press focused on the inaugural white All-Star game, remaining uninterested in the black counterpart. Typically, the *Chicago Tribune's* brief advance read "Colored Teams Play Today for Baseball Title."

For blacks, however, the game ranked as a happening of the first magnitude. The fans chose the All-Star teams—everyone had a chance to vote for personal favorites. The two largest black newspapers in the country, the *Chicago Defender* and the *Pittsburgh Courier*, conducted the voting. Players from these cities therefore dominated the squads. Still, no matter in what city he played, or the status of his team, the game afforded each athlete an opportunity to showcase his talents.

The East-West game meant glamour. The *Defender* called the occasion a "highlight in the affairs of the elite," and it provided a motive for many middle-class black fans to vacation in Chicago and stay at the Grand Hotel which also housed the ballplayers. In fact, during the days just preceding the game, the Union Pacific added extra cars on the Chicago run. The Pittsburgh train carried Gus Greenlee, eager to see seven of his Crawfords perform for the East.

The morning of September 10, 1933, dawned dark and rainy in Chicago. At game time, strong winds puffed off Lake Michigan, while lightning slashed across the sky and thunder boomed across the city. Despite the ominous weather, an enthusiastic early-afternoon crowd gathered in Comiskey Park for the big game. An exuberant Al Monroe wrote in the *Defender*, "The Depression didn't stop 'em—the rain couldn't—and so a howling mob of 20,000 souls braved an early downpour and a threatening storm to see the pick of the West's baseball players beat the pick of the East 11-7 in a Game of Games."

Black baseball's best left-hander, Willie Foster, started for the West. Leading off for the East, switch-hitting Cool Papa Bell demonstrated his fine power from the right side. Foster delivered a sizzling fastball on the first pitch and Bell wrist-snapped a towering drive to left field. Walter "Steel Arm" Davis drifted to the wall and then gave up the ball as a home run. Suddenly, a strong gust of wind pushed the ball back in the park where Davis made the catch. Assisted by the West's second baseman who booted three chances, the East still jumped off to an early lead. "Leroy Morney," wrote Monroe, "seemed to have been alone in thinking the balls were covered with moss that should not be removed."

The East led 3-1 in the bottom of the third, when little lefty Sam Streeter of the Crawfords faced George "Mule" Suttles of the Chicago American Giants with two runners aboard. A powerful man with thick wrists, Suttles could hit the ball as far as anybody, including Ruth. Over in the West's dugout, Willie Wells kept yelling, "Kick, Mule! Kick, Mule!" Streeter hung a curve, and Suttles drilled the ball out of the park in left field, shattering a taxi window across the street. Mule's smash put the West ahead 4-3.

While the East scored twice in the fifth to regain the advantage, the West tied the score twice in the sixth with back-to-back doubles. Then came Mule again. The East's manager Dick Lundy pulled Streeter and replaced him with Bertram Hunter, another Crawford. Suttles rifled Hunter's first pitch for a single, driving in the go-ahead run. The West never relinquished the lead, cruising to an 11-7 victory.

The Crawfords scheduled road exhibitions before, during, and after the NNL season. They relished big-league opposition and in 1934, following Dizzy Dean's fabulous 30-7 season with the St. Louis Cardinals, they played an exhibition series against a major-league contingent led by the zany pitcher.

Dean first tasted black medicine in York, Pennsylvania. Shortly before game time, he ambled over and did some pleading with the Crawfords. "Now listen," he said, "I just pitched two days ago, and my flipper's tired. Please take it easy on me."

"Sure, Diz, you know you can count on us," replied Josh Gibson with a sly grin.

In the very first inning, Bell opened with a vicious single and Ted Page followed with another. Dean then filled the bases drunk by passing Oscar Charleston. Next came Gibson and Dizzy served up a high fastball. Gibson's eyes opened wide, and he swatted the fat bug high and far over the center field fence.

For once, Dean stood speechless. As Gibson circled the bases, he shouted, "Hey, Diz! I said you could count on us."

The Crawfords extended their lead to 8-0 in the second inning, and Dean refused to pitch anymore, moving to second base. Meanwhile, Paige fanned 16 of the first 18 men he faced, and Pittsburgh breezed to an 11-1 victory. "They batted by ear that day," remembered Paige. "They sure couldn't see my fast one."

The Crawfords won two more in Dayton, one a brilliant pitching duel in which Paige bested Dean 1-0 in 17 innings. The two clubs next met in Yankee Stadium on a bright Sunday afternoon. Bell smashed two doubles off Dean, the second coming in the seventh inning with no score and one out. After Ted Page walked, Dean retired Charleston on an infield pop. When Gibson stepped up, a nervous Dean started screaming to the outfield, "Get back! Get back!"

From center field, Jimmy Ripple yelled, "How far do you want me to go back?" Dean just kept waving him toward the fence.

Gibson lifted a long fly to Ripple, and Bell tagged up at second. When Ripple made the catch, he raced for third. As he neared the bag, Coach

Dick Lundy gave him the stop sign. Looking over his shoulder as he ran, Bell noticed the shortstop just getting the ball from Ripple. He decided to keep going and put on a huge burst of speed, his feet skimming over the ground. He hooked home plate well before the tag.

An astonished Cool heard the umpire shout, "You're out!"

"I was safe!" yelled Bell. "It wasn't even close!"

The umpire just laughed and said, "I'm not going to let you do that against major leaguers. Maybe you can do that in *your* league, but not against major leaguers."

Oscar Charleston charged out of the dugout on the dead run, and only Gibson's enormous strength kept him from attacking the umpire. The protest served no real purpose and in the eighth, Jimmy Ripple led off with a triple and scored the winning run on a wild throw.

Always fair, always angered by prejudice, Dizzy Dean approached the umpire after the game. "Everybody knows that Bell was safe on the play at the plate," he said, "and if the Cardinals had him, along with Paige and Gibson, we could sew up the pennant by the 4th of July and spend the rest of the season fishing."

The Crawfords encountered even stronger racial prejudice off the field. Many establishments refused to serve the team. In such cases, their touring bus provided a place to sleep and eat the apples, cantaloupes and melons purchased from roadside stands.

The situation often proved less than desirable even when the team was served. "In many of the hotels," remembered Ted Page, "we had to sleep with the lights on to keep the bed bugs from coming out."

Jimmie Crutchfield tells about an incredible incident which happened between Birmingham and Montgomery when the Crawfords stopped at a roadside cafe. They approached the proprietress, who immediately started shaking her head "no."

"Why are you saying no," Crutchfield asked, "when you don't even know what we want?"

"Whatever it is, we don't have any," she replied.

"Won't you sell us some soft drinks?"

"No," she said.

One of the players asked if they could use the well—she motioned them around the building. After drinking, several of the Crawfords thanked her. She responded by smashing the drinking gourd on the stone well and muttering, "Now that you niggers have used this, it's not fit for white folks anymore."

The Crawfords enjoyed life far more at home in Pittsburgh and spent much of their leisure time at the Crawford Grille. Shunning the politicians, gangsters, and gamblers, the ballplayers formed many close friendships with the entertainers, those closest to their own lifestyle. Louis Armstrong, Fats Waller, Count Basie, Lionel Hampton, Cab Calloway, and the Mills Brothers all performed at the Grille; all enjoyed baseball. The Mills Brothers, absolutely enchanted with Paige, a fine singer and musician himself, often traveled with the club and even sported their own Pittsburgh uniforms.

The brilliant moments and good times lasted for only a short while. Despite Greenlee's determined publicity efforts, and the vibrant electricity of the team itself, the Crawfords failed to beat the Great Depression. By 1937, financial pressure began to crumble the dynasty. Seeking better money, Paige and Bell followed the sun to the Dominican Republic. A trade sent Gibson and Johnson back to the Homestead Grays, while Crutchfield went to the Newark Eagles. A knee injury forced Page's retirement. Charleston remained, an illusion of his former greatness, and the Crawfords struggled through a dismal season. When 1938 proved no better, Greenlee called it quits with baseball. After only eight years of use, Greenlee Field suffered the indignity of demolition.

The demise of the Crawfords initiated a downhill slide for Greenlee which would continue until his death. In 1950, facing a U.S. government suit for back taxes, he suffered a serious stroke. A year later, fire destroyed the Crawford Grille. Because of his physical condition, Greenlee's family never told him about the fire, and he died at his home in Pittsburgh on July 7, 1952.

Josh Gibson passed away in 1947; Oscar Charleston in 1954. Both died in the shadows of black baseball, never aware of their enshrinement by the Baseball Hall of Fame.

While most of his enormous talent also lay wasted in the shadows, Satchel Paige experienced a brief major-league career and lived to enjoy the recognition as a Hall-of-Famer. The Master died in 1982.

Cool Papa Bell is still alive, cherishing the Hall of Fame spotlight during the deep winter of his time.

Judy Johnson recently died in 1989. But at his Hall of Fame induction ceremony in 1975, perhaps Judy spoke for all the the Crawfords, and for all of the great black players of days gone by. With tears rolling down his cheeks, he said simply, "I'm so grateful."

Cool
Papa Bell

Bill Chastain

WATCHING HIM RUN was like watching a wild animal pursue its prey. He hit for power and average. But unfortunately for James "Cool Papa" Bell, he lacked one key ingredient—a lighter skin color in an era when white was acceptable and black was not. Otherwise, he would have played in the major leagues and, from all indications, flourished. Playing within his dictated parameters, Bell went on to establish himself as one of the all-time greats of the now defunct Negro Leagues.

Sure, he still remembers the frustration of the way things were, but negative thoughts do not stay in Cool Papa's head. Instead, he chooses to employ the philosophy he adopted many years past: He is blessed to smell the roses. So many were not.

Bell lives in an apartment on James "Cool Papa" Bell Boulevard in St. Louis with his wife of 60 years, Clara Bell. He is 86 years old, and he is quick to complain about failing eyesight or being slight of memory. Good pretense, but the truth be known, Cool Papa still has it. He's a wiry sort with impeccable spirit, uncanny recall, and an extraordinary sense of humor.

Living in the ghetto, Bell is prompted, on occasion, to part the living room blinds and peer out the window from his easy chair to give a safety report on my car. In between peeks, Bell sips a soda, then begins to venture back.

He began his career at the age of 17 when he followed his four brothers to St. Louis to play in a city league in 1920. Shortly thereafter he joined the St. Louis Stars.

"I was a pitcher back then," Bell says. "Threw a knuckle ball. And it was a good one. Only problem was my sister was the only one who could catch it.

"But I had a good curve ball too. I could go sidearm, three-quarters or over the top. My manager with the Stars was Bill Gatewood. He didn't want me to throw the knuckle ball, because it gave catchers fits. Gatewood finally gave me a chance to pitch in Indianapolis so I had to rely on my curve. And they had a great lineup, even had Oscar Charleston. But I was out there on the mound and had that curve ball working. Got a bunch of strikeouts in front of that big crowd.

"There was probably 10,000 or 11,000 on hand that day and the fellas on the team thought I'd be excited playing because I was so young and all. But after watching me they said I was playing like a veteran and said, 'hey, look, he's playing it c-o-o-l,' like that. So they started calling me Cool. But Gatewood said they should add something else to it so I became Cool Papa."

Gatewood realized he had a jewel in Bell, and despite the fact he was a good pitcher he knew he would be more valuable to the team as an everyday player, this according to Bell. So for the most part, Bell's pitching days ended.

He was originally a right-handed hitter, but "Candy" Jim Taylor, a man who was a player and manager for almost the entire span of the Negro Leagues, convinced Bell to switch to the left side.

"He (Taylor) said if you learn to hit from the left side, you'll have two or three more steps to first base," Bell says. "So I did it. But I wasn't real comfortable at first so I'd switch back to the right side when I got two strikes on me."

Bell notes he lost some power by switching to the left side, but it obviously didn't hurt his batting stroke as evidenced by some of the numbers he compiled during his career in Mexico, Cuba, and the Negro Leagues to name a few.

Because the Negro League games that counted were played on the weekend and the weekday games were not normally counted (rather played just to make money on attendance), the numbers credited to Bell are nowhere near an accurate reflection of what he did. According to his statistics while in the league, Bell was a lifetime .339 hitter. Perhaps his plaque in the Baseball Hall of Fame sums up his offensive accomplishments best: It says simply: "Hit over .300 regularly. Topping .400 on occasion."

Though he didn't hit a lot of home runs, he did show power at times. For example, in Cuba in 1931 when he became the first man to ever hit three home runs in one game in Cuba. The home runs came off Johnny Allen, who would later pitch for the Yankees.

As good a batsman as Bell was, it was his speed that set him apart. According to Bell, his best season stealing bases was 1933 when he stole 175 bases in just over 185 games. Many colorful stories, some true, other perhaps exaggerated, detail his blazing speed.

Among the more popular was Satchel Paige's remark: "Cool Papa Bell is so fast he can turn the lights out and get in bed before it gets dark."

An exaggeration? Not exactly according to Bell.

"We were always sleeping in these old run-down hotels and Satchel and I were rooming together on a barnstorming trip," Bell says. "I'd always go to bed early, but Satchel might stay up awhile. Anyway, there was about a three second delay in the light switch. I turned the switch off and the lights didn't go out. Second time, the lights didn't go out. My bed was right there." He points at an object no further than five feet away. "Finally, I turned it off again. Got in bed. And the lights went out.

"Satchel then had to try it. So he flipped the switch off but the lights went out." Bell offers a giggle.

Then there was the time Bell supposedly hit a ball up the middle and got hit by the ball as he was sliding into second base. Fessing up on that one, Bell just laughs. "Well, there might have been a little bit of exaggerating back then."

Rich stories of fact or fiction aside, Bell does not deny he was exceptionally fast. "I ran to first base in three seconds and circled the bases in 12," Bell says. Then with a bemused expression on his leathery face, he adds, "I guess you could say I could run a little.

"One time a fella, Fats Jenkins, told me I was the fastest he'd ever seen and asked me if I wanted to go to Europe and run. Make some real money racing. Never went though. I always wondered how I would have done.

"Was supposed to run against Jesse Owens between games of a doubleheader too. But he'd seen me run in the game. In between games they called him down from the stands. He said, 'I forgot my track shoes.'" Bell gives off a confident laugh. "I didn't have any shoes either.

"But I didn't fault him for not wanting to run against me. Because he was always expected to win by the fans. Like he would race horses for 60 years and beat 'em 'cause they hadn't really hit their stride yet. But one time they put this quarter horse out there to race against him and when they said 'take your mark' the horse got down in a stance just like Jesse." Bell demonstrates by getting up from his chair and assuming a track stance. "That horse beat Jesse by about 10 or 15 yards. I felt sorry for Jesse too. 'Cause the fans booed him for losing.

"Playing today I don't know how fast I'd be. I scored many a time from first base on a single if the outfielder didn't field it cleanly or it wasn't hit right at him. I scored from first base on a sacrifice fly. All the records I set were done on dirt. Now they play on Astro-Turf which you can run faster on."

Bell is proud of the league in which he played and its level of competition. Many times during the Negro League's existence, its players played all-star teams made up of major-leaguers in barnstorming games following the major-league season. These games meant a great deal to Bell, and to those he played with, because such games were among the only tangible comparison of talent between the two leagues. When speaking of those encounters, Bell notes: "We played tricky baseball. Not only would we hit and run, we'd also bunt and run. That's why we always did well against the white teams."

Bell always did particularly well against the white all-star teams. Recorded figures show he played against major-leaguers in 54 games, batting 215 times for an average of .391. Among the pitchers he faced were Johnny Vander Meer, Bob Lemon, Bob Feller, and the irrepressible Dizzy Dean.

At the mention of Dean, Bell giggles then sighs. "I liked old Dizzy, he was a good guy. "Like when they asked him who was the best pitcher he ever saw, Dizzy said, "Satchel Paige is the best and I'm next." Again Bell laughs. "Said if we had Satchel Paige, we wouldn't need any more pitchers."

On the subject of Paige, Bell tells of one of the cocky, but entertaining, escapades Paige performed on the mound.

"I remember one time when Josh Gibson was coming up to bat and Satchel tells him, 'I'm gonna throw three fastballs and you're not gonna hit one of them.' Then he pulled all the fielders off the field. Josh swung at the first two and the umpire called him out on the last one. Satch did this a lot of times."

The fact that the weekday games were played for entertainment and attendance rather than standing in the league often tried a player's dignity. Bell mentioned one incident when he refused to play a game on donkeys saying he was a baseball player, not a circus act. Then there was the time he had to play against a girl pitcher, but refused to follow manager Oscar Charleston's orders.

"This girl, Jackie Mitchell, was pitching against us and she'd struck out Babe Ruth and three other Yankees in another game," Bell says. "But Charleston tells me before I go up to bat, 'Look, against this girl don't hit the ball.' I said, 'Don't hit the ball? She struck out Babe Ruth.' She could throw hard enough to strike out anybody. So I was leading off and I hit a ball through the box—just missed her. It would have hurt her too. So when I came back in, Charleston said, 'Didn't I tell you not to hit the ball?' Next time up he said, 'Now go up there this time and don't hit it.' So I bunted. So I came back in and he (Charleston) says, 'Didn't I tell you not to hit it?' I said, 'I didn't, I bunted it.' He wanted me to go up there and strike out, so I finally said, 'Just take me out of the game.'"

There were a lot of second-rate trimmings playing in the Negro Leagues, but the camaraderie established because of the hard times was unsurpassed. The memories of the hard times bring quick laughter to Bell.

"There weren't a lot of places where we could eat, and we didn't have a lot of money, so we did the best we could," Bell says. "One place we went our bus broke down next to a farm. So we slept there and the next morning a man comes out and tells us he saw us broke down. Told us we could eat all the corn we wanted." Bell begins to laugh. "That was nice of him of course, 'cause we'd already eaten up half the field."

A great sense of sadness is conveyed when Bell talks of his late friend, Josh Gibson. Bell first recalled Gibson on one of his better days.

"He hit the longest ball I'd ever seen," Bell says of Gibson. "It was somewhere around New Jersey. The ball went way out of the park and into the front door of the mayor's house across the way from the ball park. The ball just missed his little baby. Would have killed it, too.

"So the mayor had to come over and stop the game. He said he had to see who could hit a ball that far and that he was going to measure it."

Bell pauses, shaking his head he continues. "Josh was like a little child. Wanted to play all the time. Later on, he had trouble with the booze. Lost all his strength. He died a weak man."

Many make a lifetime of looking back at misfortune and how they were done wrong. But for all he was denied, Bell has no regrets. Today he is poor financially, but he is a rich man otherwise. Cool Papa did indeed take time to smell the roses.

CLASH OF THE BLACK-LEAGUE TITANS

John B. Holway

WITH A PAIR OF binoculars from the stands behind first base in Yankee Stadium, you can get a close-up look at the modernistic circular stairs at the rear of the left field bull pen, some 500 feet from home plate. Look carefully. That's the spot where the longest home run ever struck in The House that Ruth Built came back to earth, like a triumphant spaceship returning from the moon, September 27, 1930. Another foot or so and it would have become the only baseball ever hit out of Yankee Stadium.

The teenage Goliath who walloped that ball—he wouldn't turn 19 for another three months—was a strapping bronze cherub from Georgia by way of Pittsburgh with only two months of big-time baseball on his record. His name was Josh Gibson.

You won't find Josh's name in any of the myriad baseball encyclopedias. And his home run is not a part of the voluminous history of major league baseball. That's because Josh was black, not white, and the team he played for, the Pittsburgh Crawfords, were in the old black major leagues, not the better known white majors.

Gibson's big Yankee Stadium blow came against Broadway Charlie Rector of the old New York Lincoln Giants, one of the best curveballers of the era. And it came in the 1930 Black League World Series—between the cocky Homestead Grays and the equally hungry Lincoln Giants.

The Grays that year were one of the greatest teams in black history—or white history, for that matter. Managing and playing first was Oscar Charleston, a leonine competitor with piercing, blazing eyes, a grip that could—and once did—wrench the steering wheel off a car, and the guts to snatch the hood off a Ku Klux Klansman or offer to throw rassler Jim Londos out a Pullman car window. All black veterans who saw him agree that Oscar Charleston was the greatest black player of all time.

Thirty-four years old in 1930, Charleston had moved to the more stationary first base after years of roaming center field in a style reminiscent of the old Tris Speaker or the modern Willie Mays. A showboat, Charleston played behind second, yet, old-timers insist, no man ever hit a line-drive over his head. Greyhound-fast and panther-savage on the bases, Charleston filed his spikes and slid in hard. He could always hit, as three years over .400 and a lifetime .352 average testify. In 1930, at the age of 34, he hit .333, bunting, spraying line drives all over the field, and pulling inside pitches over the fence in right. John McGraw called him the greatest player he'd ever seen.

A few called Charleston "the black Ty Cobb." But Oscar hit with more power than Cobb, and in the field ran circles around the slower Georgian. "Cobb," black writers sniffed, "was the white Oscar Charleston."

Grays third baseman William "Judy" Johnson was a slick fielder and line-drive hitter with a lifetime .290 average and a career high of .401 in 1929. Judy shared the team captain duties with right fielder Vic Harris, another steady .300 hitter and a slashing base runner in the Charleston mold.

At second base, George Scales was a moody player but an excellent hitter. Peppery little Paul "Country Jake" Stephens played short. Charles "Lefty" Williams was the ace of the pitching staff that year, with a perfect record of 10-0 against top black teams.

But the legend of the team was Smokey Joe Williams, the half-black, half-Indian fire baller. Smokey Joe had won his nickname in October, 1917, when he took the mound against McGraw's National League champion New York Giants and fired a no-hitter against them for 10 innings, striking out 20, only to lose 1-0 on an error. Giant right fielder Ross Youngs clapped him on the back after the game. "That was a hell of a game, Smokey," he nodded.

In all, Smokey Joe won 20 games against white big-leaguers and lost only seven. He beat Walter Johnson, Grover Alexander, Chief Bender, Rube Marquard, and Waite Hoyt, all of whom are in the Hall of Fame, while Joe still waits outside for his own ticket in. He also split two games with another Hall-of-Famer, Satchel Paige, even though Joe was 20 years older than Paige at the time. In 1930 Williams was at least 44 years old— some said 56. His real age was a constant subject of debate, a bit of showmanship that Satchel would appropriate when he himself went into the white majors.

By 1930, Smokey Joe was relegated to spot-pitching assignments. But he could still fog them in. He won seven games against other black clubs that year, lost only three. Barnstorming against the Monarchs and their lights that summer, he hooked up in one of the great classic games of black baseball lore, as 12-inning marathon in which he struck out 27 men and gave up but four hits. He finally won it in the 12th on Jake Stephens' walk, a steal, and an error.

In all, the proud Grays won 134 games in 1930 and lost but ten against all comers. They whipped even the Monarchs, the best in the West, seven straight times. That year, the Grays proclaimed themselves the kings of the black baseball world.

The only club to dispute them was the New York Lincoln Giants. Originally from Lincoln, Nebraska, the Giants had been the lords of New York for almost two decades, playing at Dyckman Oval and the Catholic Protectory (a reform school) grounds at 161st Street in the Bronx. Man for man, they thought they were just as good as the Grays, if not better.

The Lincolns were owned by a big, florid-faced Irishman and close friend of McGraw, Jim Keenan. In the winter Keenan also owned the fabled New York Renaissance club, or Rens for short, the early black basketball wizards who could whip the Celtics themselves and are today enshrined en masse in the Basketball Hall of Fame.

In fact, Lincolns left fielder and lead-off man Clarence "Fats" Jenkins played on both squads, baseball in the summer and basketball when the snows ended all baseball play. His nickname was not accurate. Jenkins was actually a deer on the bases and a .300-plus hitter at the plate. Another winter-time Ren, guard Bill Yancey, held down shortstop for the Lincolns.

The very soul and father figure of the Lincs was their venerable and beloved first baseman and manager, John Henry "Pop" Lloyd. Lloyd was 46 in 1930. Like Charleston, he had settled at the more sedentary first-base position after a lifetime of scoopin' them up at shortstop. In his heyday, Lloyd had been one of the two finest shortstops in North America. His only rival: John Peter "Honus" Wagner of the white Pittsburgh Pirates. They used to call Lloyd "the black Wagner," and Honus, out of curiosity, went to see his black eponym. "When I saw him," Wagner said, "I was flattered that they named such a great player after me." Kindly Connie Mack, the owner of the Athletics, always insisted that you could put Wagner and Lloyd in a bag together, "and whichever one you picked out, you wouldn't go wrong."

Temperamentally, Lloyd was the antithesis of Grays' manager/player

Charleston. While Charleston snarled and punched his way to supremacy, Lloyd was good-natured and gentle. In an era of illiterate, roughneck players, black and white, Lloyd's strongest oath was "Dad gum it." But he held his own, and then some, with the roughest, toughest players in the game.

In November, 1910, he was in Havana, playing the touring Detroit Tigers and their arrogant, hated, but brilliant star, Ty Cobb. The Georgian, the American League batting and base-stealing champ that year, filed his spikes and made it clear he would show these shines how to play.

The first time Cobb reached base, Lloyd was ready for him. Lloyd wore steel shinguards under his socks, and when Cobb slid into the bag on a steal, feet high and spikes flashing, Lloyd hooked a shin around Cobb's ankle and neatly flipped him into right field. Three times Cobb ran and three times little catcher Bruce Petway snapped the throw to Lloyd in time to tag him out. On the third try, Cobb saw the throw had him beat, turned abruptly and headed back to the dugout. What was even more galling, Lloyd outhit him, .500 to .369. Cobb stomped off the field, vowing never to play blacks again.

Lloyd's lifetime average against the best of the white big-leaguers was .306. In the black leagues, he frequently went over .400, ending with a lifetime mark of .343. In 1928 Lloyd hit .546. He was also tops in home runs and stolen bases that year—at the age of 44.

Charlie "Chino" Smith was the Lincolns' diminutive right fielder. ("He had Chinese-looking eyes," old-timers say in explaining his nickname.) The men who saw him agree unanimously that Smith was the greatest hitter in black ball annals. Gibson had more power, Charleston was better all-around, but for sheer hitting skills, Smitty was the best.

Smith was built along the lines of Lloyd Waner. His hitting style—spraying line drives to all fields—put one in mind of Rod Carew. Smitty had power too. In 1929 he not only hit .458 but led the league in home runs and sported a slugging average of .902, which meant he averaged almost one base every time at bat! Babe Ruth's best slugging average was .847. Appropriately, Smith hit in the Babe's number-three slot in the batting order and patrolled Ruth's spot in right field when the Yankees were on the road.

In 1930, Smitty was at his peak, not yet 30 years old. Like most black stars, Smitty was a scrapper. He would spit contemptuously at the first two pitches, tell the pitcher, "Young man, now you've got yourself in trouble," then drill the next one through the box for a base hit. Pitchers hated him.

Lincoln catcher Larry Brown was a chirpy, light-skinned bundle of energy and two-fisted toper, who almost became the first black to break into the white big leagues. The Detroit Tigers were so impressed with him that they urged him to live in Cuba for a year, learn Spanish, and come back to the States as a "Cuban." Larry figured he was too well known to get away with it. Anyway, he predicted, he and Cobb would have quickly tangled in a fight. He turned the Tigers down.

Another light-skinned Lincoln was outfielder/pitcher Luther "Red" Farrell, a .529-hitter in 1930, who, three years before, had pitched a no-hitter in the black world series, almost 30 years before Don Larsen would accomplish the same feat in the white majors.

Still another star in the Lincolns' lineup was veteran Clint Thomas in center field, a consistent .300-hitter and, according to Monte Irvin, who as a young kid saw him play, a veritable Joe DiMaggio in the field.

Lincoln owner Keenan and manager Lloyd were proud of their club. They issued a challenge to the swaggering, strutting Grays to a World Series to determine once and for all which was the greatest black team in North America. Rarely has so much power and talent been brought to-gether in a clash for the top. Even the Cardinals and Athletics, the white World Series contestants that autumn, could not outdo the drama the Lincolns and Grays brought to their grudge series.

The Series opened with a doubleheader in Pittsburgh's Forbes Field. Grays' Lefty Williams easily won the first game 9-1, his 11th straight victory—his 28th straight, including semi-pro games.

The nightcap was a wild slugfest, seesawing back and forth as runners scurried around the bases and pitchers scurried for the showers, dodging a fusillade of line drives as they ran. Young Josh Gibson contributed a triple, then uncorked a drive never seen before, a blast over the distant center field fence, some 450 feet away. No one had ever cleared that spot before, and only three men ever did it afterward: Oscar Charleston, Mickey Mantle and Dick Stuart. The Grays took a 13-8 lead after four innings, but the Lincolns forged into the lead 16-13 after seven. The Grays came back with two in the eighth, one in the ninth to tie, and one in the tenth to win 17-16.

That night the exhausted players piled into their buses for the all-night ride to New York and a Sunday doubleheader at the Lincolns' Yankee Stadium.

On Sunday, 25,000 fans were on hand to see Bill Holland try to stop the Grays' big bats. His opponent: the Ancient Wonder, Smokey Joe Williams. Each man gave up six hits. Holland spaced his six singles, one to Gibson, while Williams gave up a home run to second baseman Rev Cannady and a triple by Lloyd. The Lincolns won 6-2.

In the nightcap, Farrell of the Lincolns went against Pittsburgh's George Britt, another of the old-school, rough-and-tough players. Britt caught as well as pitched and was the peace-maker on the Grays: whenever any of the younger rowdies got to fighting under the shower or anywhere else, Britt would pull them apart, one in each hand, slam them down on the locker room benches, and tell them to cut it out. They always did.

Britt was soon locked in a great duel with Farrell. Gibson slugged a double, and the Grays took a 2-0 lead into the eighth. The Lloyd singled, Brown singled, the usually brilliant Jake Stephens muffed Yancey's ground ball to let one run in, and Britt wild-pitched a second one home and it was all tied up. In the tenth, little Jake atoned for his sin. He walked, swiped second, and when Farrell himself kicked away a ground ball, Jake raced home with the winner 3-2.

For the next three days the black world series went into a hiatus—but not the players. The Grays piled back into their bus for the ride back to Pittsburgh, where they had games scheduled every day with semi-pro teams. Posey may have had the best team in black baseball—maybe in all baseball—but he still had to pay the bills.

Thursday they rendezvoused with the Lincolns again in Philadelphia's Bigler Field, home of the black Philly Stars. Holland and Joe Williams would square off against each other once more. Both sides teed off on the two hapless pitchers. Jenkins and Thomas, the two Lincoln roommates, each slugged home runs. But Harris hit a long one for Pittsburgh, and Gibson slugged an even longer one, in fact, the longest ever hit in Bigler Field, over the roofs and across the street, and the Grays won 13-7.

On Friday, New York's forkballing Mervyn "Red" Ryan came on to tame the Pittsburgh bats and beat Britt 6-4. The Lincolns now trailed four games to two.

Saturday, September 27, 1930, the scene returned to Yankee Stadium— Farrell against Lefty Williams. In the clubhouse before the game, the Lincolns went over the Grays' lineup. "Don't give Josh nothin' inside," they emphasized. Yancey, the shortstop, was particularly emphatic on that point. ("He was scared to death of Josh," smiles Clint Thomas. "When Josh came to bat, Yancey played left field.")

Farrell nodded and obeyed and got Gibson four straight times. But it was a free-hitting game, and by the ninth, Farrell was out and Rector was on the hill. Rector must have forgotten "the book" on Gibson, because he got one over the heart of the plate, and Gibson, with "those arms like sledgehammers," in Thomas' phrase, sent the ball screaming into the sky like a golf drive toward the upper left field stands.

Johnson, sitting in the Grays' dugout behind third, swears Gibson's hit left the park completely, although from his angle the stands obscured the bullpen. Holland, in the Lincolns' first-base dugout, had a better view. He said the ball went out between the third tier and the roof, and came down against the back of the bullpen. Larry Brown, catching at home plate, concurs.

"And that was no big-league ball," says Johnson. The black leagues used a Wilson ball, unlike their more affluent white counterparts, who hit regulation Reach and Spalding balls. "If Josh had hit a big-league ball, he might have *killed* somebody," says Ted Radcliffe, another old-time player. And Johnson adds: "If that had been a big-league ball, I guess it would have ended up in the Bronx."

In all, the ball traveled an estimated 505 feet.

At the end of the inning catcher Larry Brown threw off his chest protector disgustedly in the dugout. "What'd you call for, Larry?" the Lincolns demanded.

"I called for a fast ball," Brown snapped.

"Why didn't you call for a curve?"

"God damn!" Brown exploded. "If I *knew* he was gonna hit the fast ball, I *would*-a called for a curve!"

Gibson's blow gave the Grays an 8-5 lead, with the Lincolns coming up for their last at bats. Lefty Williams walked the bases full, and Charleston beckoned old Joe Williams in from the bullpen. But pinch-hitter Julio Rojo smacked Smokey Joe's first pitch deep to right field to clear the bases and tie the game, then scored the winning run himself on Rector's single. The Lincolns had narrowed the gap to four games to three.

Rector pitched the second game, Gibson pummeled him for three more hits (no home runs), and the Grays won 7-3 to go two up again.

Sunday the two exhausted clubs walked out on the field at Yankee Stadium for one more day of battle. Another doubleheader was scheduled, and the Lincs would have to win both or it would be all over. Lloyd decided to go with his ace, Holland, who would attempt the iron-man feat of winning both games.

Old Joe Williams was his opponent in the opener, but Holland was in control. "You done hit Connie in the bullpen," he taunted Gibson, "Let's see you hit me in there now." Gibson didn't come close. He got a single in four at bats, and Holland won the game 6-2.

Holland came gamely back in game two against Britt. The Grays scored with one man on when Britt himself lifted a Texas leaguer to short right. Smith raced in, Cannady back-pedaled, and the two collided as a run scored. Smith lay motionless on the grass and had to be carried from the field unconscious. Farrell went in to replace him.

In the eighth, Holland's world caved in. Farrell let Vic Harris' drive get by him for two bases. Then he misplayed Judy Johnson's fly into a three-base error. "Holland went up in the air like an umbrella," Thomas says. Bill walked Chaney White, gave a single to Scales and a two-base hit to Gibson, and four runs were in. The Grays won the game—and the Series: 5-2.

Only one veteran of that historic 1930 series survives.

Clint Thomas went to Cuba and hit a home run off a young lefty named Fidel Castro, whereupon both men decided to retire and go into politics. Thomas became a janitor at the West Virginia statehouse. Now 87, he lives in Ashland, KY, where he is virtually blind.

Judy Johnson became a Phillies scout and coach and discovered a prospect named Rich Allen. Johnson was elected to baseball's Hall of Fame in 1975 and as a member of Cooperstown's election committee helped vote Gibson, Charleston, and Lloyd into the Hall of Fame. Johnson died June 15th, 1989.

Smith never recovered from his collision injury. He opened the '31 season with the Lincolns, but before April was over he was dead. Just what the cause was, or whether the accident had contributed to it, has never been explained.

Joe Williams finally hung up his ancient glove and spent his last years spinning stories as a bartender in Harlem, where he died in 1946.

Jenkins and Yancey were later inducted into the Basketball Hall of Fame, and Yancey served on the baseball selection committee which in 1972 named Gibson to Cooperstown. Bill died the same year Gibson was posthumously admitted.

Finally elected to baseball's Hall of Fame in 1976, Charleston's induction was noted in a two-paragraph story in the New York *Times* and a similar laconic mention in *The Sporting News*. But that was just because the white writers had never seen him and didn't know him. The few favored fans who did know Oscar Charleston knew that he may have been the greatest player ever admitted to the shrine, black or white. Charleston died of a heart attack in Philadelphia in 1954.

Lloyd retired to Atlantic City, where the local stadium bears his name, and died there in 1965. Larry Brown moved to Memphis, became an alcoholic, and died in '75. Vic Harris and George Scales moved to Los Angeles, where each died of cancer in 1978. Rev Cannady and Bill Holland lived for many years in Harlem, but have dropped from view and their present whereabouts are unknown. Jake Stephens became a deputy sheriff in York, Pennsylvania, where he died in 1981 at the age of 81, still full of pep and funny stories to the end.

Josh Gibson went on to hit an estimated 962 home runs in the next 16 years against black big-leaguers, white big-leaguers, semi-pros, Latins. That's more than 70 miles worth of home runs. Just running around the bases on them all is equivalent to a 20-mile jog.

Gibson was only 33 in 1945 when the news exploded that an unknown kid named Jackie Robinson signed to make the historic breakthrough into the white major leagues. It hurt Gibson deeply. He considered himself the king of black baseball. If anyone should be first, it should be him. Gibson took to drugs, and one bitter cold night in Pittsburgh in January 1947, just three months before Robinson's historic debut in Brooklyn, Gibson died in his sleep of an overdose.

His friends were grief-stricken. "They say Josh Gibson died of a brain hemorrhage," Ted Page says. "I say he died of a broken heart."

CHICK HAFEY'S HEARTACHES

Bob Broeg

CHARLES JAMES "CHICK" HAFEY was rangy and rapid, rawboned and rifle-armed, a Hall-of-Fame outfielder. He had two other distinctions. He was the first player to wear eyeglasses and still win a batting championship—and he held out in successive seasons until opening day and beyond.

Hafey's contractual miseries were almost as severe as a persistent sinus infection that nearly blinded him. After Chick, a three-season player at 23, hit .329 in 103 games in 1927, general manager Branch Rickey tied up the naive outfielder for $7,000, $8,000, and $9,000. Chick had three great successive seasons with the St. Louis Cardinals—1928 through 1930—when straitjacketed by a three-year contract before the Great Depression.

Shy, soft-spoken, a private person who carried a loud bat and a sly sense of humor, Chick saw nothing funny with restrictive increases after hitting .337, .338, and .336 in 1928, 1929 and 1930. The quintessence of consistency, he hit 27 homers, 29, and 26, missing more because his powerful right-handed line drives often didn't arc high enough to clear outfield fences. His runs batted in—even though the eye affliction limited him to as few as 103 of 154 games and never more than 138—were 111, 125, and 107.

After the Cardinals rallied spectacularly with 39 victories in their last 49 games to win the 1930 pennant, Chick hit a record five doubles in a losing, six-game World Series to the Philadelphia Athletics. He knew most of the Redbird regulars were making more than he, topped by second-base star Frank Frisch's $28,000. His eyes dancing with financial expectations, Chick retreated cross-country in a brand new 1929 Auburn, midnight blue with six cream-colored wheels.

Chick wrote from his Calistoga, California chicken ranch (the source of his nickname): he wanted $15,000. But the Cardinals' return offer jolted him: A mere $10,000. Besides, Chick, there's a Depression now! So Chick sat out the spring, ten days into the season, his asking price reduced to $12,500. Finally, the Cardinals capitulated, but there was a catch. He would be fined a day's salary for every game missed and for every day *until* Rickey and clubowner Sam Breadon thought he was ready to play.

Chick, assigned to work out with a farm club at Danville, Illinois, seethed, but said nothing. He let his bat do the talking. His bat and a powerful arm which captivated kids, like me, who sat in the Knothole Gang, a free-admission section for youngsters in the lower left-field grandstand. As the Cardinals romped to the 1931 pennant, capped by a Series upset over the A's, Chick nudged out incumbent batting-champion Bill Terry of the New York Giants and his own St. Louis roommate, Sunny Jim Bottomley. Chick's average for 122 games was .349.

So now he was on his 6'2", 180-pound muscle, particularly when the Giants' owner, Charley Stoneham, annoyed at Terry's request for $30,000, suggested that New York's first baseman was seeking an amount nearly equivalent to the *combined* salaries of Bottomley and Chick. Chick sought $17,500 for the deepening Depression year, 1932, noting that the amount included $2,100 deducted from him the previous spring. For the batting championship, he had been paid only $10,400, plus his World Series share, $4,474—the smallest amount paid to a winning side since 1920.

This time, trimming salaries everywhere, the Cardinals invited Chick to spring training at Bradenton, Florida, to discuss terms. When they budged at $13,000, Chick drove in white-heat anger back to California, across the Arizona desert at 90 miles an hour.

The Cardinal front office dropped a bombshell on opening day, 1932. Batting-champion Hafey was dealt to Cincinnati for two players: outfielder/first baseman Harvey Hendrick and pitcher Benny Frey, and a commodity with which Breadon and Rickey had more than a casual acquaintance—cash. H'mm, by May 10, journeyman Frey had been "sold" back to the Reds and Hendrick, better than average but no Chick, returned to the banks of the Ohio on June 5. Sure, for money.

From Cincinnati, then the Siberia of the National League, Chick got the $15,000 he'd been seeking for two years. There he joined recently supplanted former Redbirds, outfielders Taylor Douthit and Wally Roettger. But Chick was so shook up, leaving a ball club for which he'd played on four pennant-winners the last six seasons, that he "slumped" to .344. Actually, under that gnawing, poor eyesight, Chick wasn't nearly so productive at Cincinnati in four-plus seasons, actually sitting out most of 1935 and '36 with his bad eyes and a balking stomach.

At only age 33, Chick retired after the 1937 season to Calistoga, California. There, a simple man living simply and frugally, he built his holdings to 500 acres of cattle and sheep in the colorful Napa Valley country and turned over his chicken ranch to his son. If he had needed satisfaction, the 1932 Cardinals fell the farthest of any championship team—from first to sixth—the year they dealt the man who signed too long for too little.

Ever since I saw him throw and hit as a kid, then heard others talk about him in my 40 years as a baseball writer and sports editor, I became enamored of Chick Hafey, truly an unsung superstar.

Back in 1960, at a time Hafey's 25-year eligibility for election by the baseball writers was running out, I noted that he had received only 29 of 269 votes. Ahead of him in Baseball Writers' Association of America (BBWAA) balloting were Edd Roush with 146 votes, Hack Wilson and Kiki Cuyler with 72 each, Lefty O'Doul with 45, Joe Medwick with 38 and Chuck Klein with 37. Of that group, only Medwick made it with the writers his last year eligible (1968). Roush was picked in 1962, Cuyler in '68. The others were selected *after* Hafey except for O'Doul, who, like Hafey, was originally a pitcher. Obviously, they figured Lefty played the outfield as if first bounce were out.

But why, I asked Rogers Hornsby back there 27 years ago, did Hafey trail? The Rajah shook his head. "I don't know," he said. "Chick was the best right-handed hitter I ever saw."

"Sure," he continued, ticking off that list, "Wilson knocked in 190 runs one year (1930), but hell, he had guys like me on base all days. Besides, you're not supposed to pick a guy on one or two years."

So Hornsby opted for Hafey even over Medwick, though noting that if the Cardinals hadn't been so fast dealing Hafey, they could have had both sluggers in the same outfield. (Hafey's powerful arm would have been *most* impressive in the short right field in St. Louis's Sportsman's Park.) Hornsby gave only Roush an edge over Hafey. Edd is best known now for having sat out the entire 1930 season in a salary huff. Roush averaged .323, Chick .317 for their major-league careers.

Andy High went one step farther than Hornsby, labeling Hafey as second only to right-handed hitters among those he had seen. A major-league infielder from 1922 for 13 years, "Handy Andy" became long-time chief scout for the Brooklyn/Los Angeles Dodgers. He rated Hafey even over Roush.

"Not defensively, because Edd was one of the greatest ever," said High, "though Hafey was so fast and good that, yes, he played the deeper left field because of his speed. He could run a little faster, throw even better and, of course, he had more power. Even though he played at times when he almost couldn't see, he was the strongest pull-hitter I ever saw."

Pittsburgh's Pie Traynor agreed. Traynor was an early-day Brooks Robinson as a defensive star at third base. Hafey hit the ball so squarely that, as related by Burleigh Grimes, he created an illusion at bat. "If you were pitching, you actually could lose sight of the ball if he hit up the middle," said Grimes, a bulldog who threw the last legal spitball (1934).

"When I pitched batting practice," Grimes emphasized, "I always pitched Chick inside. I didn't want him to hit back through the middle."

Frank Frisch remembered a pennant-saving game in 1928, a late-season moment at Boston. With the Cardinals barely ahead of the Giants, a fast Boston veteran named Jack Smith was thrown out by Hafey when trying to score the winning run. "Greatest throw I ever saw by the best throwing outfielder I ever saw," recalled Frisch, pilot light of the Gas House Gang.

Flying once with Hall-of-Fame hitter Paul Waner of Pittsburgh, I asked if he could recall any player who matched Willie Mays for all-around brilliance. Chick Hafey, said Waner. Another time that same year, 1959, with Ernie Lombardi monitoring the press box at San Francisco, I put the same question to the big old catcher, himself bound for the Hall of Fame. Did Mays remind Lom of any player?

"If Chick Hafey had two good eyes . . . yeah, Hafey."

I'd never met Hafey, a player so well-respected yet unacknowledged. So I wrote him and expressed my desire to meet him, inviting him to see the opener of San Francisco's Candlestick Park in 1960. I included a copy of my newspaper pitch for his Hall-of-Fame potential.

I was still shaving when he knocked timidly at my hotel door. At 57, he seemed old, frail, obviously not a well man.

At breakfast, he filled me in. He'd been born in Berkeley, youngest of six brothers, three of them in the Oakland fire department and another a milk driver there. A fifth worked for a lumber mill. Chick himself had quit school in eighth grade to work in World War I.

Although he preferred football, he'd been coaxed into baseball as a pitcher by a brother because he threw so hard. He pitched when signed by the Cardinals for $250 in 1923 and was taken to camp in Florida. Yes, I'd heard it right that when Rickey, walking the outfield as combined manager/business manager with a reporter, *heard* a ball hit, he inquired who hit it. Said a gnarled assistant, Hoe Sugden, "A pitcher, Mr. Rickey, a pitcher named Chick Hafey."

Rickey corrected him. "A former pitcher. . . . Put him in the outfield."

Hafey played the outfield in 1923 at Fort Smith, Arkansas. The next year he played at Houston in the Texas League and joined the Cardinals late in the season, just in time to break an ankle in an exhibition game at New Haven, Connecticut. A year later, optioned to Syracuse, he was recalled quickly by the Cardinals and hit .302.

In the first pennant season, 1926, he won out in left field over an injured regular, Ray Blades. When Hafey was hit twice by pitched balls, the Cardinals' team surgeon, Dr. Robert F. Hyland, wondered if Hafey had trouble seeing the ball. An eye examination showed a definite weakness in the front, left eye when batting.

In recollection, Hafey never alibied. He did confirm High's memory that when his sinus problem was at its worst, he couldn't see an overhead men's room red light from one end of a Pullman car to the next. "The problem," he said, "seemed to be when the weather was coldest and brightest."

I wondered, though, if allergies, probably not nearly as fashionable or even medically acceptable in the late 20's and early 30's, could have been a factor. Hafey shrugged and smiled. "I don't know," he said, "but on those hot summer nights in St. Louis before air-conditioning, I did like to drive out into the county west of the city and sleep under a tree."

Still, two operations on his sinuses later, the suggestion that he wear glasses, then novel among athletes, helped in 1930 and '31. But from 1926 to the end 11 years later, he was magnificent under handicap, suffering a gnawing ulcer at the end as well as blurred vision. He still didn't fear the thrown ball.

"Not," he said dryly, "when you had to face, say, the Cubs' staff of Pat Malone, Charley Root, and Lon Warneke. And when I put on the glasses and hit a homer off Van Lingle Mungo at Brooklyn, Van yelled, 'That's the last time I'll respect those damned things.'"

At Candlestick I took Hafey onto the field, where the Giants were taking hitting practice. His eyes glistened behind his specs as he watched quietly until a hulking, red-faced man appeared, Tom Sheehan, the Giants' super-scout. I introduced them.

"Chick Hafey!" Sheehan exclaimed with a roar. "Damned, the man John McGraw said that with two good eyes, he'd been the best player ever. Hey, Willie, come over—"

Willie Mays came over, accepted introductions, obviously a bit bewildered because he didn't quite know the man who once had a league-tying record of ten straight hits and also eight in a doubleheader, including four doubles and two homers. As the National League's left fielder in the first All-Star in '33 at Chicago's Comiskey Park, Chick not only got a base hit, but he also did what was rare for him. He hit a savage eighth-inning line drive to *right* field off Lefty Grove, but aging Babe Ruth made a good catch at the fence.

"They ribbed me about pulling everything," Hafey said, "but they should see me play golf, which I do now and then. I got a heckuva slice. Guess I finally learned to hit to right field."

Hafey, working his ranch spread for which he had been offered 10 times the year's salary he'd paid for it, followed the game and the Cardinals only through newspapers, he said, but he watched the first game at Candlestick Park intently. When we rode back to town on the team bus, he listened, typically, more than he talked. I invited him to have dinner with me after I wrote my story at the hotel, but, no, he had his own bus to catch back home.

"I've enjoyed it," he said, softly, "it's nice to be remembered."

Remembered, indeed. Although his reward would be delayed, partly because he was limited to 13 seasons, in only seven of which he played 100 or more games, he had done enough to win Hall-of-Fame recognition. At age 67, Chick Hafey was inducted into the Hall of Fame in 1971. Remembered for his rifle arm, his bazooka bat, his ability to win a batting title with glasses and without spring training. And, yeah, remembered for the burning anger that prompted him to drive that automobile 90 miles an hour over ribbon roads 56 years ago, protesting an unsung super-star's poor pay and the bad economic timing when he wanted—and deserved—more.

SWEET DAYS OF HANK

Jay Feldman

THE NEWS OF Hank Greenberg's death in 1986 reminded me of my father's boyhood story about the Detroit Tigers' slugger and Hall-of-Famer. I called my dad that day, and asked him to tell me the tale again. Here's a memory of Hammerin' Hank in my father's own words . . .

"Hank Greenberg and I lived in the same neighborhood in the Bronx, near Crotona Park. His family lived on Fulton Avenue, which was the block adjoining the park.

"There was a nicely kept baseball diamond in the park where there were games every Saturday and Sunday—league games, semi-pro games. During the week, and also on weekends after the end of the baseball season, we kids used to use the field for pickup games. There was also a lot of lively betting on the sidelines—there were no bleachers, just a backstop, and people stood around the first base and third base lines and the outfield. The ballfield had no fences. Past the outfield there was a macadam road that ran through the park—that was considered the end of the outfield. It was about 350 feet from home plate. For somebody to hit one over that road was a good shot. Very few guys could hit it that far.

"One weekend late in the fall of 1930, after the World Series, we were out fooling around on the field. I was 12 years old. By this time, Hank was a hero in the neighborhood because that season he'd been called for a cup of coffee with the Tigers. He only got one at bat that year, but that didn't matter to us—he was Hank Greenberg, he was Jewish, his family lived on Fulton Avenue, and he was a bona fide big-league ballplayer. As it turned out, he didn't get back to the major leagues until 1933.

"But in the fall of 1930, he was the toast of the neighborhood.

"The only thing that could have been better was if he'd played for the Yankees. He had the reputation of being a really nice guy, and my friends and I used to talk about him all the time. The thing we always hoped for, of course, was that maybe sometime he would come around and play some ball with us.

"Anyway, we were out on the field this day. We didn't have enough guys for a game, so we were just shagging flies and whatnot. I was in the outfield, and I noticed this guy standing near the backstop. And even from where I was standing, I could see that he was *big*. He was wearing this raglan coat, which was the style, and he was standing there watching us. Nobody had to tell us who it was . . . everybody was saying, 'Look, there's Hank Greenberg.'

"Next thing we knew, he took his coat off, picked up a bat and started hitting. Well, every ball he hit went *way* over the macadam road. And not only far, but high—booming, towering shots. These balls were *hit*. Who could believe it?! We'd never seen shots like that!

"He hit for about an hour. A few balls were actually caught—after the first few hits, we moved back across the road. Not all of us had gloves, of course—not everybody could afford one—so there was a lot of scrambling around, with kids trying to borrow a glove. I didn't have a glove, and being left-handed, I usually played with a right-hander's glove on the wrong hand, but on this occasion I just contented myself with chasing after the balls that weren't caught. I remember thinking, 'Boy, I better not get under one of these, or it could break my hand or my head.'

"While we were running around out there, I kept thinking that I wanted to get a chance to say hello to him—nobody would have thought of asking him for an autograph—but I did think it would be nice to at least say, 'Hi, Hank.' But suddenly, without any warning, he put the bat down, waved to everybody, put his coat on and walked across the street.

"We talked about it for weeks, of course. Those of us who were there were minor celebrities. And those that weren't would say hopefully, 'Maybe he'll come again.' It was really a big deal to us. Nowadays, kids see ballplayers on TV, and players go out into the community to give clinics for kids, and they have days at the ballpark where you can come early and meet the players or take their photograph . . .

"But in those days, how many kids ever got that close—especially in their own neighborhood—to a big-leaguer?"

THE
JUDGE AND I

William N. Wallace

MY FIRST SIGNIFICANT meeting with Judge Kenesaw Mountain Landis was on a May day in 1934, when I was ten. The scene was the New York Giants' locker room in the Polo Grounds. The Judge had come to New York from his headquarters in Chicago to give the Giants the rings commemorating their World Series triumph over the Washington Senators the previous October.

He moved easily among the players, with a word here and a joke there. If he was a tyrant who inspired fear among ballplayers and most others, as some baseball historians have stated, it was not evident to me that day—or on any of the many days ahead when I would accompany him to the ballpark.

During the afternoon, I met both Horace Stoneham and Carl Hubbell. They both acknowledged me pleasantly if briefly, and Mr. Stoneham gave me a baseball signed by every one of the Giants. Then my parents took me home to Rye, New York.

(I was playing baseball in school at the time and for some stupid reason we used that autographed ball on occasion when we had lost the others in wet weeds. Finally realizing its uniqueness, I stopped such a practice but then tried to revive the signature of my hero, Hubbell, by inking over his own. The ink ran and I had a mess, rather than an autographed ball. I still have it, but no others—none with the Landis scrawl.)

I was present at the Polo Grounds that day because the Landises and my parents, Lew and Jody Wallace, were old friends, neighbors in the intimate setting of Sager's Resort on the west shore of Burt Lake, high up in Michigan's southern peninsula.

The cottage next door to ours, which Landis had built in 1905, was occupied by his daughter and son-in-law and their children, the Richard W. Phillip family from Winnetka, Illinois.

My great-grandfather General Lew Wallace from Crawfordsville, Indiana, and his son Henry, from Indianapolis, had built there on another $85 lot the year before.

When Landis, his fellow judge from Indianapolis, Albert B. Anderson, and other friends built their cottages at Burt Lake, their idea was to have a male-oriented fishing camp. By my era, though, the women had accomplished considerable interior decorating and these were no longer fishing shacks.

The Judge and Mrs. Landis usually managed a visit at least once each summer. Her proper name was Winifred but we called her for some lost reason Aunt Mim.

Because of her imposing carriage Mrs. Landis always reminded me of Margaret Dumont, the grande dame in the Marx Brothers' films, although we treated Aunt Mim with the respect Miss Dumont never got from Groucho.

The Judge, however, had some Groucho in him. He called Mrs. Landis "George" and did not mind attacking her propriety. He loved to put on an old felt hat, holed so that some white hair stuck out, and ancient fishing garb with his pants held up by safety pins. The purpose seemed to be as much to provoke George as to attain comfort.

When he arrived at Burt Lake we knew it right away. He would come across the yard—the two cottages were 100 feet away with no fencing or ground planting setting them apart—for a welcome chat and you could hear him everywhere. He could be bass, alto, and tenor all in one sentence.

My mother knew nothing of baseball and that delighted the Judge. He was "Kenny" and she was "Jody." They both loved to laugh and a sense of the bizarre was the basis of their humor. They were Indianians. So they gossiped, she giggled, and he roared.

The Judge was a commanding and dramatic person, even when his audience was only my mother and me. But he was never theatrical in the sense of being contrived or artificial. After all, he was a small-town lawyer from Logansport, Indiana, the descendant of frontier farmers who lacked any pretense.

In later years, when I read J. G. Taylor Spink's biography, *Judge Landis and Twenty-five Years of Baseball*, there was no hint of the Landis humor, no sound of his laughter. The author, the longtime publisher of *The Sporting News*, had missed the point about his subject.

By 1936, I had become a passionate fan of the New York Giants, and I'd learned a good bit about baseball. I read *The Sporting News* every week, and I understood that my summertime neighbor and by-now hero, Judge Landis, ruled the game "with an iron fist," as the scribes wrote.

That year, my Giants won the National League pennant again, setting up another so-called Subway Series with the Yankees. And the Judge invited my father and me to attend one of the games and sit with him in his box. This became a yearly custom, and, with a single exception, I attended at least one game in each Series with the Judge until his last in 1943. (The exception was the Cincinnati-Detroit Series in 1940—the only year during this stretch in which the Yankees were not the American League pennant winner.)

What was it like for a teenage baseball fan to sit with the commissioner in his front box along the first base line just off the home team's dugout for one World Series after another?

Pure heaven.

The Judge did nothing special at those games. He sat there, silent but commanding, with his chin near or on the railing fronting the box. That looked like a pose, but it was a natural posture and the subject of hundreds of news photographs during his 24 years in office.

Landis had a mass of rumpled white hair on a big head atop a small body. He was tiny, but projected power and authority. His long, lean face usually looked stern, the way a judge was supposed to look. Kenesaw Mountain Landis took a nice black-and-white picture.

The commissioner was expected to be neutral during these affairs but the first year I attended he wound up with a guest who was an unabashed, vocal Giants rooter. The elderly man in the next box, whom I later identified as Walter Briggs, Sr., the owner of the Detroit Tigers, was tickled by my enthusiasm. He chuckled and said something amusing to Landis about abuse of neutrality.

The Judge said nothing to me, and although the memory of my impolitic partisanship embarrassed me in later years, he musn't have minded too much. Or else why would he have asked me back? (As the years went by, though, I became all but invisible. I came to realize that these moments were to be retained, not assumed.)

One of the things I remember most vividly from my first World Series is that President Franklin D. Roosevelt, in an election autumn, decided to attend the Saturday game at the Polo Grounds and occupy the premier position out of the sun—the Judge's box.

The President and his entourage, amid considerable pomp and circumstance, entered the old green park by automobile. I noted his favorite specially-equipped Ford convertible and watched the entry through gates in deep center field that I'd never before seen opened. Raised as an Indiana Republican, I saw him on the field and considered him an invader of the grass territory exclusive to all but ballplayers and umpires.

The Judge, displaced to a box twenty-five feet from third base, had no comment, and I remember sitting there in the hot sun through a long afternoon as 18 Yankees, including the rookie Joe DiMaggio, rounded that bag en route to home plate.

Judge Landis had no comment either about another special World Series game I saw with him. On an afternoon in 1938, the Chicago Cubs' Dizzy Dean, his arm shot, his mouth closed and his fastball gone, held the mighty Yankees at bay for seven innings by throwing up junk. They finally got to him, though, and New York won again.

Actually, Judge Landis did once say aloud in front of me what he was thinking. It was under spectacular circumstances during the 1941 World Series between the Yankees and the Dodgers. When he was in New York, the Judge always stayed at the Roosevelt Hotel and a lunch was served in his suite before we went to the games. By custom he invited my mother and Aunt Mim had some other ladies in tow sometimes.

But on this special day it was an all-male quartet that entered the limousine for the ride to Ebbets Field.

The four were the Judge, Ford Frick (then the president of the National League and later baseball's third commissioner), I, and Perry Lesh, another youngster from Burt Lake summers who, like me, was a prep school senior.

We saw that day one of the most famous games in baseball history. The Dodgers were leading the Yankees 4-3 in the ninth when Mickey Owen, the Dodgers' catcher, dropped a third-strike pitch by Hugh Casey. Tommy Henrich, the batter, reached first and the Yankees then scored four runs to win, 7-4. I know that to be so because I have to this day the program for the occasion, and I scored the game immaculately in black ink.

We were all moved by the sudden turn of events, no one more so than the Judge. On the way back to Manhattan, in the limousine, Landis kept repeating, to Frick, or to me or to no one in particular, "That poor young man, that poor young man."

The language seemed stiff to me. Mickey Owen, up to then, was no poor young man but a tough 25-year-old Missouri farmer who caught well and carried a huge chew in his cheek. But the Judge's display of compassion for a player on the field impressed me deeply.

Of course, Landis was known as the players' commissioner. I knew he had compassion for them off the field when they were kept "chained" in the farm systems of the St. Louis Cardinals or the Detroit Tigers. He released dozens of players from those farm systems by declaring them free agents.

But how about black players? Why did he do nothing for them?

Murray Polner, who wrote a biography of Branch Rickey in 1982, claimed that Landis did nothing to end segregation in organized baseball when he might have, and even put an occasional barrier in the way. Polner substantiates his views in part although I see some misinterpretation. I will argue with the historians during my time at bat.

A later commissioner, a football man named Pete Rozelle whom I came to know, admire, and like, spoke in June 1987 to the Associated Press sports editors convention about the lack of black head coaches in the National Football League.

Rozelle deplored the situation, but said it was a matter not on his agenda. He said it was up to the club owners, who do the hiring and firing, to resolve the problem.

Landis said exactly the same thing in my hearing, although not to media folk. He was answering a question, put by Arthur Slaughter, my family's chauffeur and a black man.

It was outside Yankee Stadium in 1942, and the World Series matched the Cardinals and the Yankees. The United States was deep in World War II and blacks as well as whites were making a mighty effort.

Perhaps that is why Art Slaughter chose then to ask his question. Slaughter knew the Judge from 20 years at Burt Lake and he was a friend of the Landises' chauffeur. The three mixed, had fished, got along well. He bluntly said, "Judge, when are you going to let the colored ballplayer in the major leagues?"

The Judge replied in his fiery way, "I can't do any damn thing about it, Art. It's up to the club owners."

That was that for then and Slaughter went away. Art lived to see Jackie Robinson play in the majors, but the Judge did not.

My last Series with the Judge was in 1943. That was a grim, wartime fall. I was a private first class in the Army by then, but I was stationed at Bethlehem, Pennsylvania, so I could get to Yankee Stadium to watch the Yankees take on the Cardinals again.

My father, mother, and sisters, never enthralled by baseball, begged off; Aunt Mim was absent and so was Charles Hughes. The Judge was stuck with extra tickets. So he gave them away to soldiers and sailors, enlisted men he found outside the stadium. "Here," he said.

The next year, 1944, I passed through St. Louis at World Series time, on furlough from Camp Polk in Louisiana. I had wired ahead to Landis's office in Chicago to make my probable presence known. Leslie O'Connor, his longtime aide, replied that the Judge was too ill to attend that Series, between the Browns and the Cardinals, but I would be welcome nonetheless. I passed on O'Connor's kind invitation. For me a World Series without the Judge was unacceptable.

Late that fall Landis died in Chicago, the day before I boarded a troop ship for England. He was 78, I was 20.

.303 IN 1930

Mark Van Overloop

THE GOLDEN DECADE of the 1920s has been called the "most prolific decade of hitting in baseball history." The years 1921 through 1930 saw both leagues have yearly averages of at least .280 for the entire decade. And in 1930, the National League batted its way to the unmatched average of .303.

There are a number of factors to which the league's exceptional 1930 average can be attributed. The first and foremost reason would seem to be that 1930 was the peak year of the lively ball era. After the 1919 season, the manufacture of baseballs used by the major leagues began using more efficient yarn-winding machines. This tighter-wound yarn resulted in a much livelier ball with greater resilience. With the birth of the lively-ball era in 1920, the scales were tilted in favor of the hitters.

Why has such an outstanding season not happened since? One reason is that the ball itself was made less lively after the National League's monumental 1930 season. Also, "baseball gradually became a harder game to play (especially to hit)." But the primary difference was the rise of the art of pitching.

First, starting pitchers presently pitch basically every fifth game, instead of every third or fourth day, as was the case in the past. Therefore, with fewer starts, starters have stronger and fresher arms for their appearances. Second, the development and widespread use of the "slider," which combined the speed of a fastball with the breaking of a curve, gave batters yet another tough pitch to battle. Third, much greater emphasis was placed on relief pitchers. The greater reliance on relief specialists can be shown by the fact that in 1930, National League teams averaged 13 saves apiece. This figure was almost triple by 1980, as each team had an average of

1930 TEAM'S AVERAGE
AND THEIR NUMBER OF REGULARS OVER .300

TEAM	BATTING AVERAGE	REGULARS OVER .300
New York Giants	.319	6
Philadelphia Phillies	.315	5
St. Louis Cardinals	.314	8 (all)
Chicago Cubs	.309	5
Brooklyn Dodgers	.304	5
Pittsburgh Pirates	.303	6
Boston Braves	.281	4
Cincinnati Reds	.281	4

37 each. The batters now must face a steady stream of strong, fresh, rested pitchers as starters are pulled out of the games earlier and the relievers (often more than one) enter sooner. In 1930, National League teams averaged 66 complete games apiece, which is over 2½ times what the number of complete games had shrunk to by 1980—just 25 per team.

Other factors made life more difficult for post-1930 batters. With the introduction of night ball games in 1935, the ball became harder for batters to follow at night.

Coast-to-coast travel by plane resulted in player jet-lag. When the leagues expanded to cities beyond the Mississippi River onto the West Coast, they could no longer recover during the extra time it took to travel between cities by train.

Better fielding became the result of improved equipment. Longer fingers and deeper pockets made the gloves larger, enabling fielders to reach more balls.

Major-league baseball talent was diluted by the expansion of both

NATIONAL LEAGUE'S ASCENDING BATTING AVERAGE PLATEAUS

PLATEAU	AVERAGE	SEASON
.270—.79	.279	1900
.280—.89	.289	1921
.290—.99	.292	1922
.300—	.303	1930
High after 1930	.279	1934

leagues. When major-league baseball expanded from 16 to 26 teams, the talent was gradually spread out to cover the ten new teams.

The one inescapable conclusion to be drawn from the 1930 National League season was that the hitters were vastly superior to the pitchers. The league's .303 average, the highest league batting average in the major leagues in this century was, in large part, responsible for the league's 4.97 earned run average—the worst ERA for the National League since 1900. There were more talented hitters (17 future Hall-of-Famers) than star pitchers (only four of whom would win election to Cooperstown) playing in the league that season. Striking fear into the hearts of those National League pitchers were hitters the likes of George Sisler, Rabbit Maranville, Gabby Hartnett, Frankie Frisch, Jim Bottomley, Chick Hafey, Cuyler, Wilson, Teray, Lindstrom, Ott, Traynor, the Waners, Heilmann and Klein. Forty-seven (83%) out of the National League's 56 primary pitchers had ERAs beyond 4.00, and 21 (37%) of these were over 5.00 as well. All eight teams had ERAs over 4.00, with two teams over 5.00 and another team even over 6.00. With pitching staffs giving up better than an average of five or six runs per nine innings, the teams' hitters had the burden of trying to outscore these high run totals.

In addition, there was less relief pitching, both in quality and in quantity in 1930. Therefore, starting pitchers often pitched into the late innings, giving up more hits and runs as they tired. Three of the all-time top ten base hits in a season totals were collected in 1930: Bill Terry,

National Batting Averages Since 1900—by Decades

DECADE	BATTING AVERAGE
1900-09	.255
1910-19	.256
1920-29	.285
1930	.303
1930-39	.277
1940-49	.260
1950-59	.260
1960-69	.252
1970-79	.256
1980-89	.259

254 (tied for second), Chuck Klein, 250 (tied for fifth), and Babe Herman, 241 (tied for ninth). The league's eight teams scored 7,025 runs which averages out to 878 per team—the highest run scoring in the major leagues in the 20th century. The 11.4 total runs (5.7 per each team) scored per game is also the most in this century. The pennant-winning Cardinals averaged over six runs a game in becoming the first team ever to score 1,000 (1,004) runs in a season.

The *last team* to bat even .300 was the 1950 Boston Red Sox who hit .302. League averages hit rock bottom in 1968 when the American League hit all of .230, with the highest team average a lowly .240. Only one (regular) player hit .300, as Carl Yazstremski led the league with a not-too-healthy .301 mark.

One question to ponder: Do great hitters make a great year? Or does a great year—with many factors favoring the hitters—make the hitters appear great? As for 1930, the great hitters simply overwhelmed the pitchers. Many of these hitters had career seasons (the best season of an individual career) all in the same year and most of the rest had either very good or, at the very least, good seasons in 1930. The proof is in the pudding: an amazing 25% (16 out of 64 regulars) of all 1930 National League regulars would eventually gain entrance to the Hall of Fame.

HUBBELL'S GREATEST GAME

John M. Rosenburg

THE BROOKLYN DODGERS' Charlie Dressen dubbed him the "Meal Ticket." And from 1928 to 1943, that's what the great left-hander Carl Hubbell was for the New York Giants—a meal ticket. And a good one. For in those years, by coupling one pitch with pin-point control, Hubbell won 253 games, making him the Giants' most effective hurler since the immortal Christy Mathewson. In addition, he established a series of records that would be the envy of almost any pitcher in the majors.

In fact, there are many who consider Hubbell among the top two or three southpaws of all time. And no wonder. Look at some of his accomplishments:

- He once won 24 games in a row—16 from the middle to the end of the 1936 season, and eight from the start of the following season, a record;
- He also pitched 45⅓ innings without giving up a run, a record for left-handers;
- In May of 1929, Hubbell racked up a no-hit, no-run game against the Pittsburgh Pirates;
- In seven seasons he had an earned run average under 3.00—during one season, he hurled ten shutouts;
- Hubbell was also the mainstay of the Giant pitching staff when New York won pennants in 1933, '36, and '37 with seasonal records of 23-12, 26-6, and 22-8 respectively;
- The lanky, grey-eyed left-hander also won not one, but *two* Most Valuable Player awards, a difficult trick for a player who's not out there performing every day.

Hubbell was late in coming to the big leagues, primarily because

Detroit's Ty Cobb, his first manager in the majors, warned him during spring training in 1926 not to use the "screwball," his best pitch. Cobb and others insisted Hubbell would ruin his arm with his unnatural delivery, an inward twist of the wrist. (He eventually did, but not before he finished a fairly normal career.)

Without the screwball, Hubbell was ineffective and knocked around the minor leagues for five years. He was about to quit baseball when the Detroit organization released him to Beaumont of the Texas League.

Claude Roberts, the manager at Beaumont, told Hubbell, "If you want to use the screwball, go ahead and use it."

Hubbell did. Before long his impressive work at Beaumont led to a contract with the Giants, then managed by John McGraw. Hubbell was then 25 years old.

But, when old-timers get together and the conversation drifts around to Hubbell, elected to the Hall of Fame in 1947, there's always that perennial question: Of all the great games pitched by King Carl, the Giants' "Meal Ticket," which was his greatest?

Was it, as many claim, his magnificent performance in the second All-Star game in 1934? Certainly, that one has to be high on the list.

Bill Terry was the manager for the National League All-Stars that memorable day. His opponent was Joe Cronin, manager of the Washington Senators.

No one was surprised when Terry called on the 6'1", 175-pound Hubbell to hurl the first three innings for the Nationals. After all, he had just received an award as the outstanding player in the National League for the previous season.

Hubbell, however, didn't have a very outstanding start. Charley Gehringer, the first man up, singled and went to second when outfielder Wally Berger juggled the ball. Hubbell then did what, for him, was highly unusual: he walked Heinie Manush. That little slip brought him face to face with none other than George Herman Ruth—the Sultan of Swat and hero of the first All-Star game. At that point, no one could have imagined the drama that was about to unfold.

It began with Hubbell throwing four pitches to Ruth—the first one a ball, the next three, strikes.

The next hitter was another fearsome slugger, the Yankees' Lou Gehrig. Again, Hubbell's first pitch was a ball. But again, the next three were strikes. On the third, Gehringer and Manush pulled a double steal.

Now, the A's Jimmy Foxx came to bat. A single here would mean two runs, but Hubbell, as always under fire, remained calm. This time, the first pitch was a strike. The second was fouled off. The third, a screwball, sent "Ole Double X" down swinging.

In the next inning, with the Nationals now leading 1-0 on a homer Frankie Frisch banged off Vernon "Lefty" Gomez, Hubbell had yet to face two more of the American League's heaviest hitters—Al Simmons and Joe Cronin.

The great left-hander struck out both.

Bill Dickey, the next batter, singled and that brought Gomez to the plate. The first pitch to Gomez was a strike. So was the second. This time, the bat flew out of Gomez' hands toward second base.

"Leave it there Lefty," Frisch yelled at Gomez. "You won't need it." He was right. Gomez took a third strike to end King Carl's three-inning stint.

In consecutive order, Carl Hubbell struck out five of baseball's most powerful hitters. Of the 15 pitches he threw to that awesome quintet, only one—the foul by Foxx—was touched by a bat.

"Unquestionably, that was the greatest pitching performance I have ever seen," Joe Cronin said later.

But what about the Meal Ticket's classic effort against the St. Louis Cardinals at the Polo Grounds on July 2, 1933? This was no three-inning assignment. This one lasted 18 innings! Hubbell and the Red Birds' Tex Carleton hooked up in one of the greatest pitching duels of all time before more than 50,000 tense fans.

With the score 0-0, Jess Haines replaced a tired Carleton in the 17th.

In the 18th, the Giants scored a run on a single by Hughie Critz, giving Hubbell a hard-earned 1-0 victory. Six hits and no walks. And in 12 of 18 innings, not a single Cardinal reached base.

Was that Hub's greatest game? Some think so.

Let's take a look at the first game of a doubleheader between the Giants and Dodgers on Memorial Day, 1940, which was played in that homey little park called Ebbets Field. No one could have written a better scenario for this, the most intense rivalry in baseball.

As the Giants crossed the river to Brooklyn, the Dodgers were in first place in a close race with the Cincinnati Reds, while the Giants were in a respectable third.

To make sure the Brooklyn "Bums" would stay where they were, Dodger fans began lining up outside the park before midnight. When the gates opened at 1:30 a.m., 5,000 poured into the stands. By 11 a.m. the gates had to be closed as almost 35,000 had squeezed into the Brooklyn band box, including more than 300 standees. The police said more than 20,000 were turned away. In addition to the play on the diamond, the day would be highlighted by barrages of grapefruit, oranges, and paper, all aimed at the Giants.

Opposing Hubbell in that opening game was Luke Hamlin, but Luke ran into trouble immediately, hitting a batter and giving up a single, a double, and two walks. Three Giant runs were the result.

But it was early in the game and Dodgerdom was convinced its heroes could get the three runs back and more. So when Hubbell came out of the Giants' dugout for his first turn on the mound, Dodger fans whooped fiercely for a rally. Unperturbed, Hubbell retired the side in order.

In the second inning, the Dodgers sent Van Lingle Mungo to the hill and it began to look like a pitcher's battle from then on.

Second baseman Johnny Hudson got the Dodgers' hopes up when he singled off Hubbell in the third.

The next batter, Brooklyn catcher Gus Mancuso, slugged a screamer down the right field line that brought everyone roaring out of their seats and sent Hudson flying around the bases.

It was foul by inches.

While the Dodger rooters settled back with loud groans and Giant fans sighed in relief, Hubbell took a stretch and fired to Mancuso again. The big catcher swung lustily, but the result was a weak roller to the mound. Hubbell scooped the ball up, pivoted, and fired to second to start a double play that was completed easily.

There was no more scoring until the fifth, when the Giants punched three hits to score two more runs, making it 5-0.

Mancuso revived Dodger hopes briefly in the sixth with a high drive to center field. But Frank Demaree gathered it in for an out and another scoreless Brooklyn inning.

Center fielder Dixie Walker, called "The Peoples Cherce" by the inimitable Brooklynites, tried to bunt his way on in the seventh, but was thrown out by Hubbell. Another goose egg went up on the board.

In the next inning, Dodger first baseman Dolf Camilli lined a shot to right field. Mel Ott caught it easily.

The Giants scored once more in the top of the ninth on a double, an error, and Hubbell's fly ball to Joe Gallagher in right field. That made it 7-0 New York.

The only action in the Brooklyn half of the ninth was a bunt by Hudson that Hubbell again turned into a quick out.

With that loss, the Dodgers slipped to second place. And Carl Owen Hubbell, a gritty southpaw with a high kick of the right leg and a deadly overhand delivery, went into the history books with another masterpiece.

Hubbell had faced the minimum number of batters—27.

He gave up no walks, striking out six.

Only three batters put the ball out of the infield in fair ground (Hudson with a ground single, and Camilli and Mancuso, each with a fly ball).

But think of this—in setting the Dodgers down that day, Hubbell threw only 81 pitches. That's an average of nine an inning, or three per batter.

Clearly, this was King Carl at his best.

CARL OWEN HUBBELL'S MAJOR LEAGUE RECORD: NEW YORK GIANTS 1928–1943

Games	535
Innings Pitched	3,589
Wins	253
Losses	154
Winning Percentage	.622
Hits	3,463
Runs	1,380
Earned Runs	1,188
Strike Outs	1,678
Bases on Balls	724
Earned Run Average	2.97

HUBBELL'S WORLD SERIES RECORD:
1933, 1936, 1937

Games	6
Wins	4
Losses	2
Winning Percentage	.667
Innings Pitched	50⅓
Bases on Balls	12
Strike Outs	32
Earned Run Average	1.79

TEN NO-HITTERS
FOR FELLER?

John B. Holway

IT'S BEEN OVER half a century since the dimple-chinned farm boy, Bobby Feller, pitched his first game in a Cleveland Indian uniform in 1936. He was 17 years old, the model for Roy Hobbs, "The Natural," who learned his baseball from his father in the cornfields of Iowa.

Bobby's first game was an exhibition against the St. Louis Cardinals. Frank Frisch, the Cardinals' playing manager, took one look at Bobby warming up and took himself out of the lineup. Shortstop Leo Durocher hugged the water cooler and had to be dragged, kicking and screaming, to the batter's box. Bobby faced nine Cardinals that day and whiffed eight of them.

It took a long time to brush all the hayseed out of his hair, however. Catcher Billy Sullivan was eight years older than Bobby and had been assigned to room with the kid. He remembers Bobby wearing an old-fashioned white nightgown and practicing autographing baseballs. (Little did Sullivan then realize how quickly those autographs would become valuable.)

Another roommate, second baseman Roy Hughes, remembers the two of them taking in the sights of New Orleans; they'd bought two nickel bags of peanuts and strolled around the French Quarter munching them. In the hotel, Roy says, Bobby propped a pillow up on the bed, got across the room, and burned fastballs into it by the hour. "You couldn't go to sleep," Hughes laughs, "listening to that *plop! plop!* all night long."

Bobby Feller would become the Nolan Ryan of the 1930s and '40s, and until Ryan came along in the '70s, Feller held the modern record for strikeouts—348 in 1946—and no-hitters—three in his career. He surely would have had even more of each if he hadn't lost the four top years of his career to duty in World War II. But even with the war, Feller threw 12 one-hitters, more than any other man. All told, Feller's 15 low-hit games—no-hitters plus one-hitters—were a record (since broken by Nolan Ryan). Feller always insisted he had more stuff in some of his one-hitters. Let's take a look at each of his 12 one-hit games that came oh-so-close to the elusive no-hit.

NUMBER ONE—CLEVELAND: APRIL 20, 1938

Feller was just 19, beginning his second full year in the majors. He was coming off a 9-7 season the year before, when he had struck out a man an inning, a difficult feat in those days when batters didn't swing for the fences as much as they do now.

Feller was facing the St. Louis Browns at old League Park. The Browns were hitless through five innings. In the sixth, Feller's old roommate, Billy Sullivan, strode to bat. This was the first time the two had faced each other as opponents. Sullivan, a left-handed hitter, occasionally liked to bunt between first and second to force the right side of the infield to play in, giving him more room to hit into the outfield. Feller, of course, knew this.

In the sixth, Sullivan did bunt. "I figured, he'll be looking for me to drag bunt, so I intentionally gave it away, because I knew he'd break toward first." That's just what happened. As Feller's follow-through carried his body to the first-base side of the mound, Sullivan bunted behind him, toward short. Feller, off balance, recovered, reached the ball a split second late, and fired it to Hal Trosky at first.

"It was mighty close," Trosky said after the game. "If I'd been the umpire, I'd have hated to call it. But I thought we had him. I thought the ball was in my glove while his foot was still in the air."

The umpire thought differently. He spread his palms, gesturing safe.

Sullivan was sorry about it. "As long as we had to lose anyway, I wish you'd gotten your no-hitter," he told Feller.

Today Sullivan recalls, "I got hate mail about it from lots of people for a number of years."

"It could have been called either way," Feller says today. "They called him safe, and that was that."

Feller won the game 9-0, with ten strikeouts. He went on to win 17 and lost 11, with 240 strikeouts, best ever for someone that young.

NUMBER TWO—BOSTON: MAY 25, 1939

Red Sox manager Joe Cronin may have to share some of the responsibility for costing Feller his second shot at a no-hitter. Sox second baseman

Bobby Doerr was having trouble hitting Feller and went to the veteran Cronin for help. The only way to hit Feller, Cronin advised, was to divide the plate into "zones,"—and swing only at pitches in those zones there he could get the bat around quickest.

In the second inning, Doerr hit what Feller calls "a broken bat bloop over the first baseman's head. It landed right on the line" for a single.

Feller got some revenge by striking Cronin out two times on his way to ten whiffs. The Sox's hot rookie, Ted Williams, went 0 for 4.

NUMBER THREE—CLEVELAND: JUNE 27, 1939

In the first night game ever played in Municipal Stadium, Feller took the field against Detroit before 55,000 fans who were hoping their unpredictable phenom would do something dramatic.

Feller quickly raised their excitement level in the first inning. He gunned down his former teammate, Earl Averill, on "the fastest ball I've seen in my 11 years in the big leagues." Averill took a cut at it, but "it was in catcher Rollie Hemsley's glove before I got my bat half-way around."

In the fifth, Averill came up again. This time, "I threw him a half-speed ball," Feller said later, and "he met it solidly."

It was the only hit Detroit got all night. Averill apologized later and said the hit "doesn't make me happy," especially since he was the second ex-teammate to cost Feller a no-hitter in just over a year.

Feller, however, "was not chagrined," one reporter wrote. He went on to whiff 13 Tigers and walked three in winning 5-0. Hank Greenburg fanned three times.

Feller went on to win 24 and lose nine for the year, while striking out a league-leading 246. The next April—opening day—Feller finally got his elusive no-hitter, over the White Sox.

NUMBER FOUR—PHILADELPHIA: JULY 12, 1940

Only 8,000 fans turned out, the smallest crowd to see an American League night game up to that point. For seven innings Feller made them glad they'd come, setting the Athletics down without a hit.

As he and catcher Hemsley walked to the dugout together after the seventh, Feller showed him a blister on the middle finger of his pitching hand. That probably cost him another no-hitter.

A's first baseman Dick Siebert led off the eighth. Siebert was a notorious first-ball hitter, and Hemsley ordinarily would have called for a curve to start him off. But, because of the blister, Rollie signaled one finger for a fastball instead. "If I hadn't known about the blister, I never would have called for a fastball," Hemsley said afterwards.

Siebert swung on it and slapped a grounder toward second. "It was an easy ground ball through the box," Feller says now. He feels he should have made a play on it, but it skipped through him and into center field, less than a foot from Ray Mack's glove. "It just snuck in there," he says.

Feller won the game 1-0 on 13 strikeouts and three walks. He would end the year with 261 K's and 27 victories.

NUMBER FIVE—ST. LOUIS: SEPTEMBER 26, 1941

Hitler's Wehrmacht and Stalin's divisions were mopping up in Poland as Feller went out to start the second game of a doubleheader, seeking his 25th victory.

For four innings he held the Brownies hitless. In the fifth, he walked Johnny Berardino. Rick Ferrell then stepped in. "Feller was the toughest for me to hit," says Ferrell, now a Tiger executive and Hall-of-Famer. "I've been asked that many times. I always say, 'Bob Feller.'"

With two strikes on him, Ferrell hit "a swinging bunt down the third-base line," he recalls. "I was swinging at the ball and topped it. I didn't mean to do it, it just happened. It rolled out in front of the plate down the third-base line.

"I fell off to the left of the mound and was slow fielding the ball," Feller recalls. He made an off-balance heave to first and threw the ball into right field, as Ferrell chugged all the way to second. The scorer called it a hit and an error. After pitcher Denny Galehouse walked to load the bases, the infield was back as Johnny Lucadello hit a grounder and Berardino scored. Harlond Clift then sent a long fly to score Ferrell for the second run.

Today Feller shrugs—"It was my fault."

"Bob and I often laugh about that one," Ferrell says. "He said, 'That was a hell of a hit you had.' I said, 'Yeah, if you could field worth a damn, you could have had a no-hitter.'"

Feller won the game 3-2, fanning six. He didn't know it yet, but Pearl Harbor lay just over two months in the future. By New Year's, Feller would be in the Navy. He would not pitch another game for almost four years.

NUMBER SIX—CLEVELAND: SEPTEMBER 19, 1945

Now a combat veteran of the South Pacific, Feller had just returned to the Indians and was looking for his fourth victory. About 4,500 chilled fans shivered in old League Park.

This time the villain was Detroit's Jimmy Outlaw. In the fifth, he swung on a fastball and hit what he calls a "poop" single over shortstop. "It wasn't hit too good," he admits.

"It was a flub-a-dub," Feller agrees, "one of those dying quails."

Les Fleming, a first baseman playing left field that day, misjudged the ball. "He should have caught it easily," Feller says. "He started back on the ball, then came in, but he didn't come in quickly enough. If he'd just stood still, it was hit right where he'd been standing." Instead, the ball dropped in front of him for a hit.

Feller won 2-0, with seven strikeouts and four walks and ended with a 5-3 mark for the year. The following spring he got his second no-hitter, against the Yankees.

NUMBER SEVEN—CLEVELAND: JULY 31, 1946

Pitching with only two days' rest, Feller was looking for his 20th victory against the league-leading Red Sox.

He was wild that day, walking nine men, beginning with lead-off man Wally Moses in the first. Moses took third on ground balls by Johnny Pesky and Ted Williams. Big Rudy York drew a second base on balls, and Moses scored on a double steal.

In the top of the second, Feller came up with two men on and tripled them both home.

His old nemesis, Doerr, led off the second. This time he got around on the pitch better than he had back in '39 and pulled the ball on a line into left field for a hit. For the second time he had just spoiled Feller's no-hit bid. "It was a clean hit," Feller says. He won the game 4-1, with nine strikeouts.

NUMBER EIGHT—CHICAGO: AUGUST 8, 1946

Eight days after his one-hitter, Feller opened a doubleheader against the White Sox. He was on a strikeout pace that would bring him 348 whiffs for the year.

Again, it was a former teammate, catcher Frankie Hayes, who cost Feller a no-hitter. Hayes, a .212 hitter, led off the seventh with a weak, looping Texas-leaguer to left. "It was one of those handle hits," Feller says. Shortstop Lou Boudreau drifted back, calling, "I've got it, I've got it." But the wind kept carrying the ball back over his head. At the last second, Lou stopped and yelled, "Take it," to left fielder Pat Seerey. Seerey, however, was nowhere around. He had failed to come in after hearing Boudreau call,

"I've got it." "He was standing there with his hands on his hips," Feller says. The ball dropped between him and Boudreau.

Feller won his ninth shutout of the year, however. He would go on to win 26 games, ten of them shutouts.

NUMBER NINE—CLEVELAND: APRIL 22, 1947

Only 2,629 fans came out in 45-degree weather to see Feller oppose the Browns at Municipal Stadium. Today Feller says he doesn't remember this game at all.

He had good control that day, walking only one man and striking out ten. Hitting against a Hall-of-Famer like Feller "is such a challenge," says Brownie outfielder Al "Zeke" Zarilla, now living in Hawaii. "It gives you a lift to hit against pitchers like that." Feller had a curve "that was outstanding when it snapped over." And, of course, "he threw so hard, you just couldn't pick up the spin on the ball. I think he struck me out the first two times at bat. Usually I don't strike out too many times, about 30 times a year."

But in the seventh, a curve "just hung outside—it was actually probably out of the strike zone," Zarilla says. "It didn't have the snap on it like it usually does. When you hit against Bob, you have to take advantage of it. I kind of arched it over the shortstop's head, just out of everyone's reach."

It was Feller's ninth one-hitter. By now the newspapers were getting blase and gave hardly any space to the feat.

NUMBER TEN—CLEVELAND: MAY 2, 1947

It had been just ten days since the previous one-hitter when Feller faced the Red Sox, seeking his third shutout in a row. He got lead-off man Dom DiMaggio. Then little Johnny Pesky, a left-hander, swung late on a fastball ("It had to be a fastball," Pesky says, "he didn't want to put me on ahead of Ted Williams") and lined it into the opposite field for a hit. Williams then smacked into a double play.

Feller went on to win 2-0, with ten strikeouts. Again the newspapers yawned. He won 20 that year and led the league in whiffs again.

Feller would not pitch another one-hitter for almost five years. But he did get his third no-hitter, against Detroit in 1951.

NUMBER ELEVEN—ST. LOUIS: APRIL 23, 1952

Feller, 33 years old, had made a great comeback the year before, when he was 22-8 with the second-place Indians. His opponent, Bob "Sugar"

Cain of the Browns, had won 11 with the fifth-place Tigers the year before. Interestingly, Cain had been the losing pitcher two years earlier when Feller had pitched his third no-hit game, and was also the victim in 1951 when Cleveland's Bob Lemon beat him with a one-hitter. "I figured I owed them one," Cain would say.

Spring training in Florida had been beset with bad weather. But Cain considered it a blessing. Instead of pitching in exhibitions, he did a lot of running. "I've never been as well trained before," he said.

Both Bobs were making their second starts of the season, and each was looking for his second win. Feller's victory had been a shutout over Detroit. He would be pitching without his regular catcher, Jim Hegan, who had handled his 1951 no-hitter, and without Larry Doby, an excellent fly-chaser, in center field. The veteran Birdie Tebbetts was behind the plate. Pete Reiser, the ex-Dodger, was in center, and rookie Jim Fridley went to left.

Pitching before the home fans in 47-degree, overcoat weather, Cain struck out the side in the first. Then Feller took the mound against left-handed lead-off man Bobby Young, a life-long consistent .250 hitter. The first pitch was a curve for a called strike. Feller made what he would call his only bad pitch of the night—he decided to waste a pitch.

"I was throwing for the outside and got the ball too close to the alley," and Young hit a long, curving fly to the left. Fridley appeared to misjudge the spin on the ball. He broke to his right, then reversed to his left, and finally the ball sailed over his head, as Young legged it all the way to third.

"Fridley should have caught it," Feller says simply.

Marty Marion followed with a ground ball to third, which Al Rosen booted, and Young raced across the plate.

In the second, big Luke Easter blasted a Cain pitch 400 feet into the wind, only to see it caught at the warning track. In the fifth, Easter broke up Cain's no-hitter with a clean single into center, Al Rosen walked, Fridley missed a bunt then popped up, and Cain ended the threat by getting Ray Boone on a double play.

Feller, meanwhile, got the next 17 men in a row, after Rosen's error, until Bob finally walked two men. But he finished the game by facing 28 official batters in a row without giving a hit.

In the last of the ninth, however, Cain was still holding onto the 1-0 lead when he struck out Harry "Suitcase" Simpson for the final out.

It was Feller's 11th one-hitter, the only one of the 11 broken up by an extra base hit and the only one he lost.

It was also only the second double-one-hitter ever pitched. The only other one had come 47 years earlier, July 4, 1906, when Pittsburgh's Lefty Leifield dueled Chicago's great Mordecai Brown. Leifield himself got the only hit off Brown when he beat out a sacrifice, but Brown won it 1-0, helped by four Pittsburgh errors.

Five days after his duel with Cain, Feller would be blasted for 18 hits by the Athletics, but Fridley gave him six hits and Rosen gave him three home runs, as Bob went all nine innings to win 21-9. He would win only seven games more and lose 12 more to end up with nine victories and (like Leifield) 13 losses for the second-place Indians, the worst season of his career to that point.

NUMBER TWELVE—CLEVELAND: MAY 1, 1955

Feller, 36, was coming off a 13-3 year in '54 and had lost his first decision in '55. The old hop was gone from his fastball—he was down to one strikeout every two or three innings now—but he was getting by on intelligence and finesse. This was his chance for one last hurrah.

Feller pitched the first game of a Sunday doubleheader against the Red Sox, who had already broken up three of his no-hitters. He wasn't the overpowering Feller of his youth, but Boston catcher Sammy White says, "Even in his late years, he was still tough. You couldn't see him—hard to pick up." Feller struck out two men that day but walked only one.

Again it was a catcher who spoiled it, and again the fateful hit came in the seventh. White, a right-hander, hit a one-out fastball on the end of his bat "and just looped it over the shortstop's head."

"It was a good clean single," Feller admits.

"Very embarrassing," White says, "I broke my bat."

Feller would win only three more games in his career. In the second game that afternoon he watched from the dugout as the new phenom, 22-year-old Herb Score, beat the Sox with 16 strikeouts.

To pitch a no-hitter, Feller says, "you've got to be a little lucky." For one thing, "it depends on what kind of hitters you're pitching against. The strikeouts tell a little more about the hitters. So there are a lot of factors, not all of them in the record books."

When he finally turned in his toeplate, Feller had pitched three no-hitters and 12 one-hitters. Only five of the one-hitters were clean hits. He might just as easily have ended up with ten no-hitters and five one-hitters.

FELLER'S 15 LOW-HIT GAMES:

YEAR	OPPONENT	RANK	BA	BROKEN UP BY	BA	BB	SO
1938	St. Louis	7	.281	Sullivan	.277	5	10
1939	Boston §	2	.291*	Doerr	.318	6	13
1939	Detroit	5	.279	Averill	.262	3	13
1940	Chicago	4(tied)	.278	NO HIT	—	5	8
1940	Philadelphia §	8	.271	Siebert	.286	3	13
1941	St. Louis §	6(tied)	.266	R. Ferrell	.252	7	6
1945	Detroit	1	.256	Outlaw	.271	4	7
1946	New York	3	.248	NO HIT	—	5	11
1946	Boston	1	.271*	Doerr	.271	9	9
1946	Chicago §	5	.257	Hayes	.212	3	5
1947	St. Louis	8	.241	Zarilla	.224	1	10
1947	Boston	3	.265	Pesky	.324	1	4
1951	Detroit	5	.265	NO HIT	—	3	5
1952	St. Louis §	7•	.250	Young	.247	3	5
1955	Boston	4	.264	White	.261	1	2

§ away   *led league
• St. Louis finished seventh but at the time of this game was in first with a 7-1 record.

HISTORY'S LOW-HIT PITCHERS

NAME	NO-HITS	ONE-HITS	TOTAL
Nolan Ryan	5	11	16
Bob Feller	3	12	15
Addie Joss	2	7	9
Old Hoss Radbourn	1	7	8
Jim Maloney	3	5	8
Grover Alexander	1	5	6
Mordecai Brown	1	5	6
Sandy Koufax	4	2	6
Tom Seaver	1	5	6
Steve Carlton	0	6	6
Don Sutton	0	5	5

WHEN
OWNERS REIGNED

W. G. Nicholson

THE 1930s AND 1940s were especially difficult times for major-league baseball players. Most were underpaid, and all—including the game's biggest stars—were exploited by capricious and greedy baseball owners and general managers. Hard as it may be to believe, conditions were so bad for players that some existed on relief payments during the off-season. Meanwhile, Branch Rickey in 1942 earned in excess of $100,000 as general manager of the St. Louis Cardinals.

In the winter of 1941, Rickey's celebrated battle with the Cardinals' Johnny Mize was typical of how management dealt with players. Mize in 1940 had done it all: he led the National League with 43 homeruns (a team record), 137 runs batted in, and a slugging average of .636. At the end of the season, however, his salary was cut. Why? Very simply, his batting average had fallen to .314 from the previous year's .349. After fierce bargaining, Mize finally signed in 1941 for his restored 1940 salary of $7,500. But his was a Pyrrhic victory. Regarded as an ungrateful malcontent, the National League's most feared slugger was traded at the end of the year to the New York Giants.

Although Babe Ruth, who earned $80,000 a year in 1930, was richly compensated for his considerable skills, most major-league players were exploited by management during the first half of the century. Chick Hafey, who from 1928 through 1930 did not bat under .337 or drive in fewer than 107 runs a season, was offered his old salary of $10,000 for the 1931 season by the St. Louis Cardinal management. The future Hall-of-Famer held out in the spring of 1931 for $15,000 and eventually signed for $12,500, but $2,100 was deducted because the fleet outfielder was not ready to play at the beginning of the season! After leading the National League in batting with a .349 average in 1931, Hafey once again asked for $15,000, which quickly earned him a trade to Cincinnati, then regarded as the Siberia of baseball.

In 1930 Hack Wilson set the National League record for homeruns (56) and the major-league record for runs batted in (190) while batting .356. He earned $33,000 in 1932, but then his salary was cut to $7,500 by the Cubs in 1933, an unbelievable drop but not an unusual one in a period when there was no limit as to how much a player's salary could be cut from one year to the next. Wes Ferrell, who in 1932 had earned $18,000 for winning 23 games, the fourth year in a row that he had won 21 or more games for the Cleveland Indians, was, incredibly enough, offered a contract of $11,000 for the next year. It is not at all surprising that major-league players became as adamant as they did about maximum salary cuts during the 1950s.

Hafey, Wilson, and Ferrell were, of course, among the superstars of the 1930s; the treatment of average and marginal players was even worse, with many earning salaries of no more than $3,000 or $4,000 a year. The St. Louis Browns were embarrassed by a newspaper story in the winter of 1939-40 which revealed that three Brownies—shortstop Johnny Berardino, outfielder Joe Glenn, and pitcher Ed Cole—were on public assistance, each receiving $15 a week in the off-season.

Joe DiMaggio and Yankee management repeatedly clashed over salary during the 1930s and 1940s. The Yankee great earned $37,500 in 1941, the year he batted .357, hit 30 homeruns, drove in 125 runs, and hit in a record 56 consecutive games. And how did management reward that exceptional performance? Ed Barrow, the Yankee general manager, offered DiMaggio a 1942 contract calling for $35,000, justifying the $2,500 cut with the excuse "there's a war on." DiMaggio eventually signed a more generous contract and after World War II became the first major-league player to earn $100,000 a year. (It was not until 1958 that St. Louis' Stan Musial received the National League's first $100,000 salary.)

There was no shrewder general manager than the Cardinals' Branch Rickey. Receiving 25% of the profits made from the sale of players from the prolific farm system he had established, Rickey earned $42,340 in 1937. By 1942, his last year in St. Louis before moving on to the Brooklyn Dodgers, Rickey's salary was $80,000; in addition, at that time he received a 20% share from the sale of each player contract. The St. Louis Cardinals' Sam

Breadon, perhaps the most self-serving of the major-league presidents, in 1942 paid himself a base salary of $100,000 before sharing in his team's considerable profits.

Soon after the advent of World War II, most of baseball's high-priced stars were in uniform, and major-league rosters were increasingly filled with aged and draft-deferred players. In an attempt to forestall inflation, Washington urged employers throughout the nation to put a lid on salaries, dictating specifically that a professional baseball player would request a raise if he could convince his team and the Internal Revenue Service that he merited one. In 1943 the minimum major-league baseball salary was set at $3,500, with no player earning a salary higher than that paid by his team in 1942. Moreover, players were urged to hold defense-related jobs in the off-season and to contribute 10% of their salary towards the purchase of war bonds and stamps.

Baseball owners were quick to respond. Dutch Leonard, who had won 18 games for the seventh-place Senators the year before, asked for a raise in 1942. Clark Griffith, the Senators' owner, turned him down with the admonition that "In these war times, anybody ought to welcome the same salary he received last year." The Detroit Tigers proved to be even more "patriotic" by offering $11,000 salaries for 1942 both to pitcher Buck Newsom and to first baseman Randy York, a $21,500 cut for the former and a $9,000 cut for the latter.

The Cardinals' rookie Ernie White won 17 games for St. Louis in 1941, while losing only seven en route to compiling a 2.40 earned run average. In the World Series that October, he threw a shutout in his only appearance against the Yankees. The young South Carolinian knew his $3,300 1941 salary had been a real bargain for Breadon, but White asked for only a $900 raise to $4,200. Incredibly enough, he had to settle for $3,800 in 1942, a measly $500 raise. Not surprisingly, with policies such as these, the average major-league salary between 1939 and 1943 declined from $7,306 to $6,423.

Major-league umpires as well as players were grossly underpaid during the 1930s and 1940s. Bill McGowan, in 1944, was the highest paid umpire in the American League; after 21 years in the majors he earned a mere $9,000 a year. George Pipgras and Eddie Rommel, two other outstanding arbiters, were each paid $6,000 after eight years of major-league service.

Major-league attendance fell during the first part of World War II, but in 1945 a new record was set when 10,847,123—more than 700,000 over the old mark set in 1930—paid to see an inferior version of the game during the war years. Even the St. Louis Browns, one of the majors' least successful teams, made a profit of $250,000 in 1944 on a gross income of $550,000. Due in large part to management's tight-fisted policies, the most financially successful National League team in the 1940s was Sam Breadon's Cardinals.

By the spring of 1944, a number of players who had been encouraged by owners to take off-season jobs in war industries chose to remain in relatively high-paying blue-collar work, rather than earn a few dollars more playing baseball and face the taunts of fans accusing them of draft-dodging. In December of 1944, Branch Rickey addressed this new manpower problem facing the major leagues when he said, "I don't think any players, even those engaged in defense work, will refuse to return to baseball because of a question of salary." How wrong he was. Virtually every team had three or four persistent holdouts in 1945 who eventually forced salaries to rise a bit.

The most celebrated of the wartime holdouts were the Cooper brothers: pitcher Mort had won 21 or more games for three years from 1942 to 1944, and Walker, his catcher, had batted .317 in 1944. Pleading first that he could not exceed $12,000 during the wartime wage freeze, Breadon offered the Coopers $12,000 each. Then he tried to embarrass them by telling reporters that "At a time like this, it is unwise for players who have been excused from military service for some reason or another to publicize their dissatisfaction with the contracts which have been sent them." Later, after unsuccessfully trying to play the Coopers off against another holdout, shortstop Marty Marion, Breadon reluctantly offered the brothers $15,000.

Although his brother accepted Breadon's offer, Walker Cooper flatly refused the raise, telling the owner, "You told me you couldn't pay us more because of government regulations." Breadon responded angrily, "You're mule-headed." "And you," said Cooper, "were a liar." It's no wonder that Walker was soon sold to the Giants, never again to play for the Cardinals, while his then sore-armed brother Mort was fobbed off to the unsuspecting Braves.

With the end of World War II in the summer of 1945, virtually all of the many major-leaguers who had been in the armed forces were on hand for spring training in 1946, anxious to resume their careers and to earn as much as they could. Jorge Pasqual and his brothers were more than willing to oblige American players by luring them with huge salaries that spring to their newly-formed Mexican League. Commissioner Happy Chandler quickly warned potential deserters that they would be suspended if they did not return to their American teams by Opening Day and would be banned for five years if they signed Mexican League contracts. More than a dozen major-leaguers, however, succumbed to Pasqual's blandishments and elected to play in Mexico.

Among them was Max Lanier, the fine Cardinal pitcher who had won 17 games his last full year before entering the service. Lanier was looking for a contract of slightly more than $10,000; Breadon, however, offered him only a $500 raise over his 1944 salary. The disgruntled 30-year-old pitcher then accepted Pasqual's offer of $20,000 a year for five years, along with a $25,000 signing bonus.

The departure of a significant number of talented players to Mexico gave Breadon and his fellow owners pause. Stan Musial, who had batted .347 and .357 in his last two seasons before heading off to war, had signed a St. Louis contract for $13,500 before Jorge Pasqual offered him $175,000 for five years. Alarmed over the possible loss of Musial, Breadon grudgingly gave the Cardinal star a $5,000 raise two months after the 1946 season began, and a $31,000 contract for 1947.

A greater threat than the Pasqual brothers emerged in 1946 with the formation of the American Baseball Guild, a fledgling union headed by Robert Murphy, a Boston attorney and Harvard Law School graduate, who set out to organize players for collective bargaining. Murphy's attempts to unionize baseball failed in the summer of 1946, partly as a result of attitudes represented by Pittsburgh's Paul Waner who said, "Guilds have no place in baseball. I was in the big leagues for 20 years and never once figured I was being underpaid or mistreated. Baseball is very generous and has kept quite a number of fellows from pushing plows for a living."

But in spite of the Paul Waners of baseball, major-league owners were not unmindful of the threats posed by unionization and the Mexican League. The owners formed a committee in 1946 which met with player representatives to deal with the major grievances. Out of these meetings came a $5,000 minimum salary, a 25% pay cut limit in a single year, and provisions for a rudimentary pension plan. These relatively modest gains, however, were not significantly altered for the next 20 years. During that period, there was little question that the owners remained dominant.

Marvin Miller and effective unionization arrived in 1966, but players did not begin to make significant financial gains until two events transpired: in 1972, the players, much to the surprise of the owners, stood together during a 13-day strike over a pension dispute; and in 1975 Andy Messersmith and Dave McNally challenged the renewal option clause in the uniform players contract. The minimum salary, after all, was but $6,000 in 1967, a gain of only $1,000 since 1946. It jumped to $12,000 in 1970, to $21,000 in 1978, and to $60,000 in 1986. Paralleling those gains, the average major-league salary in 1966 was $19,000, $99,876 in 1978, $241,497 in 1983, and $410,732 in 1987. Approximately 60 major-league players earned salaries in excess of $1,000,000 a year in 1986.

TED'S
ALL-STAR HUNCH

John B. Holway

THE NEWSPAPERS SCREAMED of war in Europe as the players hailed cabs to Detroit's Briggs Stadium. Already two big leaguers, Hank Greenburg and Hugh Mulcahey, had been drafted. Pearl Harbor was a mere five months away.

This was to be the last pre-war All-Star game, and it would turn out to be one of the most dramatic of all time, thanks to the heroics of a player who would soon be flying combat missions for the Marines.

Ted Williams then was a spindly 22-year-old on his way to what remains major-league baseball's last .400 season. This was Ted's second All-Star game. He hadn't been chosen in 1939, his rookie year, even though he was hitting .300 and would go on to lead the league in RBI's. In '40 he had gone 0-for-2, as the Nationals won 4-0, their third victory in the first eight games.

In 1941, Ted was hitting .405 at game time. Yet he was overshadowed by Joe DiMaggio, who six days before had knocked a homer over Ted's head in Yankee Stadium to pass Willie Keeler's record hitting in 44 straight games. Joe's streak had reached 48 by the All-Star break.

In their first at bats, against Brooklyn's Whitlow Wyatt, Joe fouled out, and Ted, hitting clean-up, walked.

In the fourth inning, against big Paul Derringer of Cincinnati, Cecil Travis doubled, DiMaggio hit a 415-foot fly to Pete Reiser in center, and Ted lashed a line drive over Bob Elliott's head in right for a double to knock in the game's first run.

Cincinnati's Bucky Walters, now pitching for the Nationals, opened the sixth with a double. Stan Hack sacrificed him to third, and Terry Moore hit a long fly to Williams at the base of the left field stands. There seemed no chance to catch Walters at the plate, but Ted's tremendous throw almost nipped Bucky. The score was tied 1-1.

In the botton of the sixth, Walters walked DiMaggio, Williams hit a long drive but he didn't pull it enough and Reiser caught it in right-center. Jeff Heath walked and Lou Boudreau scored DiMaggio with a single to make it 2-1.

In the seventh, Enos Slaughter singled to left and took second on a Williams error. Shortstop Arky Vaughan had been sidelined for a week with a bruised heel and was not scheduled to start, but he had insisted on playing. He had hit only four home runs so far this season, but now he lined one into the upper deck to put the Nationals ahead 3-2.

National League manager Bill McKechnie stuck to his game plan of changing pitchers every two innings and brought in right-hander Claude Passeau of Chicago to start the seventh.

Passeau threw a natural slider, a common pitch today, but a novelty then. "Only two or three in the league had a pitch like that," says Passeau from his home in Mississippi. "The ball just sailed. I don't know how I did it, it was just a natural pitch. The fastballs would sail in on left-handed hitters. I could get left-handers out where I couldn't get right-handers. I pitched to left-handers high inside. It would just sail in on the thin part of their bats. Slaughter, Johnny Mize, Mel Ott, they would put their good bats back in the rack and tell the bat boy, 'Go put 'em in the clubhouse, we don't want to break them.'" Passeau calls the slider "my out pitch. If it hadn't been for that, I wouldn't be up there."

Passeau got lefty Bill Dickey on a line drive to third. Another lefty, Charlie Keller, the American League home run leader, took a terrific swing at a slider and missed for strike three. Joe Gordon, a right-hander, also went out, giving Passeau an impressive one-two-three inning.

In the Nationals' eighth, Johnny Mize doubled, and, after Slaughter was called out on strikes, Vaughan came up again. Out in left field, Williams had a hunch that Arky might park another one. "I get funny hunches that way," he said later. "I never say anything about them, and as sure as I do, they don't come true."

Sure enough, Vaughan did knock another into the upper deck, making the score 5-2 and making Vaughan the first man ever to hit two homers in one All-Star game.

In the bottom of the eighth, Travis, a lefty, went out. DiMaggio, hitless all day, hit Passeau's slider for a double, and the left-handed Williams came up with a chance to get one run back for the Americans.

Passeau got two strikes on him and threw him the slider, low. Ted took the pitch and Babe Pinelli, a National League umpire, raised his thumb and waved Williams out. "A National League strike," Ted would say later.

Losing by three runs and with only four outs left in the game, Williams had another one of his hunches. "I had a funny feeling I was going to get up there at least one more time and hit one," he said. "I figured I was going to get up there again. I was as sure of it as anything."

Ted must have been the only one in the park who thought so.

Dom DiMaggio, a righty, smacked a single to score his brother and make it 5-3. Boudreau, another righty, also singled, and the mighty Jimmie Foxx, the only man besides Babe Ruth with 500 lifetime homers, stepped in to hit. Passeau had gotten the lefties with his slider, but the right-handers were hitting him. Foxx was the most powerful right-hander in the majors. Passeau bore down and got him swinging on three pitches.

That may have been the turning point of the game.

Passeau had pitched two days earlier in the regular season, and his arm was getting stiff. He had completed his two innings, and Carl Hubbell was in the bullpen, warmed up and ready to pitch in the ninth. Hubbell was a lefty, and Williams hated "cutesy" left-handers, especially those, like Hubbell, whom he had never seen before. He says he hit .317 lifetime against lefties, compared to about .355 against right-handers.

But catcher Harry "the Horse" Danning liked what he'd been seeing of Passeau's slider. "You stay in," he suggested. McKechnie agreed. Hubbell sat back down in the bullpen.

In the ninth, Vaughan, the hero of the game, didn't take the field. McKechnie put in Eddie Miller, the best fielding shortstop in baseball, to give the Nationals defensive insurance.

The first batter, right-hander Frankie Hayes, popped to Billy Herman, the future Hall-of-Fame second baseman playing his record eighth All-Star game. Fans began filing out the exits.

Right-handed Ken Keltner pinch-hit a tricky grounder to Miller, who got a glove on it but couldn't make the throw. A lucky break for the Americans.

Joe Gordon, another righty, lined a single to right-center. The fans stopped at the exits to watch.

Cecil Travis walked to load the bases, and the great DiMaggio was advancing to the plate with one out. The noise in the stands began to swell.

Joe took his wide stance, hands at his ear, bat pointing straight up, and waited, motionless, impassive. He fouled off a pitch, took a vicious cut at the second and missed it by a foot. Passeau then challenged him with another strike, and Joe slapped it straight to Miller. Double play all the way.

Eddie handled it easily and flipped to Herman. A 90-foot throw and the game would be over. Billy whirled—and threw it 12 feet down the line, pulling big Frank McCormick off the bag. DiMaggio, who had slowed down, speeded up and crossed the bag safely, as Keltner scored to make it 5-4.

Did Travis take Herman out of the play? Herman denies it. "It was a double play ground ball," he says simply and honestly. "Travis didn't touch me. We just didn't complete it, that's all."

Passeau is philosophical. "'Herman was one of the best second basemen I ever saw. He said he just fancy-danned. Like he said, 'I was shinin'.'"

By rights, Passeau should have been in the clubhouse. Instead he had a one run lead, two outs, two men on, and tall Ted Williams walking to the plate.

The question was obvious: Should Passeau walk Williams, putting the winning run on second, and pitch to Dom DiMaggio? The infielders gathered around and urged him to pitch to Ted. McKechnie nodded. Apparently they all thought Claude could get him out again with the slider.

Ted had been swinging late all day and was determined to get in front this time. "I was nervous," he said later, "but I was bearing down a little harder than I ever did in my life."

Passeau's first pitch was low. Ball one. Ted swung at the second, but he was too far out in front and drilled a foul down the first-base line. Strike one. The third pitch sailed high and inside, and Ted took it. Ball two.

Then the slider again, the same pitch Ted had struck out on a few minutes before. But this time it was high. "The ball got away from me," Passeau says. "The instant it left my hand, I knew I was a dead duck."

"It was fast and about elbow-high," Ted said. "I said to myself, 'This is it.' I shut my eyes and swung."

The ball zoomed up into a stiff crosswind, while the crowd cheered, then gasped as it appeared the wind would carry it foul. It didn't.

Slaughter, the right fielder, just put his hands on his hips and turned his back on the stands, as the ball climbed to the top of the roof, struck a red, white and blue bunting, hung there for a moment, and dropped to the field.

"It didn't miss by much going over the whole works," Keltner says. "Another three or four feet and it would have cleared the press boxes."

"A towering shot," agrees pitcher Sid Hudson. "You knew it was gone as soon as he hit it. Everybody in the park knew it. Ted knew it too. He started clapping his hands."

Ted watched the ball battle the wind for a few seconds, then he shot into the air with a whoop and began galloping and leaping around the bases, not running but frolicking, gamboling, frisking, jumping.

A mob of players was waiting at home plate. His manager, Joe Cronin, "half crazed with delight," pulled his cap off, whacked him on the head, mussed his hair, hugged him. "Ted's grin could be seen from the bleachers," one reporter wrote, as Ted hobbled to the dugout with the whole American League team on his back. A fan reached down and snatched his cap. Ted grabbed it back and disappeared into the runway to the clubhouse.

The National Leaguers watched dazedly. "He's just inhuman," Mc-Kechnie muttered. Passeau was disconsolate but defiant. He's still defiant today.

"I kind of laugh about it," Passeau says from his retirement home in Mississippi. "He didn't hit the ball good, not real well at all. It was a short pop-up fly." Detroit's right field foul line is only 325 feet away, and the upper stands hang out over the field only 318 feet from home. "Don't get me wrong, no alibi," Passeau says, "but any other park, it would have been a big out."

From his fishing home in Florida, Williams agrees. "It wasn't all that tremendously hit," he admits. "It was high and looked like it was going a mile. Actually, it was a big high fly. In most parks it would not have been a home run, even though I hit it way up on the facade."

Actually, the ball surely would have been a home run in Yankee Stadium, the Polo Grounds, Ebbets Field, Sportsman's Park in St. Louis, or League Park in Cleveland. It might have gone out of almost every other park except Fenway Park and Cleveland's Municipal Stadium. Slaughter, who caught the ball when it fell back onto the field (and still has it in his home), just clucks his tongue and points out, "It's pretty daggone high there."

In the American League clubhouse, players jostled each other to punch Ted playfully and slap him on the rump as flashbulbs popped. Even his enemies of the press box relented and enjoyed the moment with him. Largely because of his tiffs with the press, Williams had recently threatened to quit the game and enjoy the idyllic life of a fireman. One Detroit paper ran this headline the next day:

FIREMAN COMES THROUGH

New York Daily Mirror columnist Dan Parker headlined his column:

TED WILLIAMS STILL TOPS OUR Di MADGE

And the *Boston Herald* proclaimed:

TED THE KING
SUCCESSOR TO
RUTH'S ROBES

This was the first, and grandest, of four All-Star homers Williams would smash. Only Stan Musial, with six, would surpass him. And of the 128 home runs smacked in a half-century of All-Star games, Ted's towering blast to the roof of Briggs Stadium is still the most dramatic and unforgettable of all.

TRIP TO THE BIG LEAGUES

Bob Fulton

JOE NUXHALL WAS so petrified that day in 1944 he tripped and fell flat on his face en route to the mound. Moments later he uncorked a warm-up pitch that clanked off the screen behind home plate.

It was hardly a promising start to his major-league career. But then, Nuxhall was no ordinary major leaguer. He was a nervous—an understandably nervous—15-year-old.

Nuxhall won 135 games in a career that spanned 16 seasons, but the left-hander's most celebrated moment in the majors was indisputably his first. Nuxhall pitched two-thirds of an inning for manager Bill McKechnie's Cincinnati Reds against St. Louis on June 10, 1944, to become the youngest big-league player ever. It's a distinction he holds to this day.

"That was only the fifth or sixth major-league game I'd ever seen," recalled Nuxhall, now in his 21st season as a Reds broadcaster. "I was just sitting there [in the dugout] like a spectator. All of a sudden Mr. McKechnie said, 'Joe, warm up.'"

The Cardinals, headed for a third consecutive 100-win season and their fifth world championship, owned a commanding 13-0 lead by the time Nuxhall entered the game in the ninth inning. When he departed nine batters later, five more runs had scored and Nuxhall, though it likely afforded him little solace at the time, was assured a niche in baseball history.

His place in the record book came about by accident. The Reds were actually interested in another pitching prospect named Nuxhall—Joe's father, Orville. A Cincinnati scout dispatched to watch the elder Nuxhall throw unwittingly discovered the son after asking a bystander, "Where's Nuxhall pitching?" He was directed to a field where Joe's municipal league team was playing. Impressed by the youngster's fastball, the scout suggested a tryout at Crosley Field. When Nuxhall passed muster, the Reds signed their pitching prodigy to a contract.

The aquisition of a player so young would have seemed an extraordinary measure in any but those extraordinary times. Because of World War II and the resulting exodus of players into the military, baseball was suffering from an acute manpower shortage.

The quality of play dipped accordingly, yet major-league baseball continued to operate with encouragement from President Franklin Roosevelt, who perceived the national pastime as a morale-booster. The doors were thereby opened to players who, but for the aberration that was wartime baseball, would have reached the majors much later, if at all.

Time magazine noted that "rosters were as full of unknown names as YMCA hotel registers." Teams searched frantically for able-bodied recruits; some weren't even *that* particular. Some teams, such as Leo Durocher's 1944 Brooklyn club, featured a motley assortment of callow rookies and wizened veterans: four Dodgers were 18 or younger and three had celebrated their 40th birthdays (meaning they were older than their manager). Graybeards were teamed with players who were still learning how to properly hold a razor—if they had begun to shave at all. Carl Scheib was 16 when he made his pitching debut with the Philadelphia A's in 1943 and 16-year-old Tommy Brown played in 46 games at shortstop for the Dodgers a year later. But none of the wartime *wunderkinder* was as young—and few were ultimately as successful—as Nuxhall. He developed into a solid major-league pitcher, in spite of a debut that inspired comparison with the *Titanic*.

There was little doubt, even at 15, that Nuxhall possessed the physical tools to win in the majors. What's more, his dimensions (6'3", 193 pounds) worked to his advantage on the mound and also served to minimize his teammates' teasing, to which, as a rookie, he was inevitably subjected.

"They were all pretty good about it," said Nuxhall, at that time a recent graduate of Wilson Junior High School in his hometown of Hamilton, Ohio, not far from Cincinnati. "Like [outfielder] Eric Tipton said, I was big enough to kill a bear with a switch."

That might have proved a far less formidable task that the one he faced against St. Louis, when McKechnie, fearing the Cardinal onslaught would deplete his pitching staff for the next day's doubleheader, ordered Nuxhall to warm up.

"I was scared to death just warming up," Nuxhall recalls. "Then I tripped over the step in the dugout [on the way to the mound for the ninth], right in front of everybody. I fell flat on my face."

The schoolboy pitcher wasn't alone in his unease. The Cardinals watched with mounting trepidation as Nuxhall demonstrated an alarming lack of control with his warm-up pitches, exemplified by one toss that sailed over the head of catcher Joe Just and ricocheted off the screen behind home plate.

Nuxhall explains what happened to him on the mound: "I got the first guy out on a ground ball. I went 3-2 on the second guy before he walked. The third guy popped out. I got a ball and two strikes on the next hitter [Debs Garms] . . . then I realized where I was." Nuxhall, consequently, came unglued. As he emphasized to a reporter later in his career, "A couple of days before I'd been pitching to 13-year-olds."

After Garms trotted to first with a walk, the reality of the situation struck Nuxhall like a slap in the face. For approaching the plate was Stan Musial, the previous year's batting champion and MVP, a player who unnerved even veteran pitchers as he assumed his characteristic corkscrew stance. Musial's chief recollection of the moment is tht Nuxhall "couldn't understand why he was out there." Nuxhall might have wondered why, too, after grooving a fastball.

"He hit a frozen rope," Nuxhall recalls. "I can still see that ball zooming by."

Musial and his teammates knew they were feasting off a rookie, of course, but they were unaware that the victim of their assault was a record setter. "We didn't know he was 15 years old, didn't hear it mentioned even," ways former St. Louis shortstop Marty Marion, the National League MVP that season.

St. Louis left fielder Danny Litwhiler, like many of his teammates, cast a wary glance at Nuxhall as he stepped into the batter's box. "He could throw hard, but he didn't know where it was going. Neither did I," recalls Litwhiler, now a minor-league batting instructor with Cincinnati. "I don't know who was scared the most, me or Joe. He threw about six pitches and walked me. I never lifted the bat off my shoulder."

After that base on balls forced in a run, pinch-hitter Emil Verban singled in two more to pad the lead to 18-0. Six consecutive batters had reached base. Someone else would have to nail down the final out, McKechnie decided. He ambled to the mound and, addressing Nuxhall, said gently, "Well son, I guess you've had enough."

That statement signaled the end of a major-league debut that was anything but auspicious. Before the media even had time to make a fuss over the majors' youngest player, he was gone. Within days of his debut, Nuxhall was shipped to Birmingham of the Southern Association; he would not pitch in the big leagues again for eight years.

In 1952, Cincinnati gave Nuxhall another shot at the big leagues. It's somewhat ironic that Nuxhall's spot of the Cincinnati staff was secured during a 19-1 loss to the Dodgers, a rout that must have evoked haunting memories of a similar lopsided defeat in his youth. Only this time Nuxhall was superb.

"The Dodgers scored 15 runs in the first inning, 12 after two were out," says Nuxhall. "I got into the game in the fourth. I pitched four shutout innings. That made it for me. Gabe Paul, the general manager at the time, told me I would've gone back to the minors if I had pitched poorly."

Nuxhall's scoreless performance at cozy Ebbets Field effectively canceled his ticket back to the bushes. He would lead Cincinnati with 17 victories and the National League with five shutouts in 1955, would be selected to two All-Star games, would finish his career in 1966 with a fine 135-117 record. But those achievements will forever be overshadowed by the fuzzy-cheeked, 15-year-old Nuxhall who controlled his nerves about as well as his pitches.

THE MYTH OF PESKY'S THROW

John B. Holway

BASEBALL LOVES ITS MYTHS and clings to them passionately—DiMaggio's hitting streak, Branch Rickey as the Great Emancipator, Lou Boudreau's invention of the shift. And one of its favorite myths is that Johnny Pesky held the ball in the seventh game of the 1946 World Series while Enos Slaughter raced home with the run that won the Series. Today people who never saw the Pesky play—who hadn't even been born until years later—believe the myth without question: "Pesky choked" . . . "The Red Sox choked" . . . "The Red Sox always choke in the big ones."

But it just isn't so. Pesky never held the ball.

"John got a bad rap," says the Cardinals' "Mr. Shortstop," Marty Marion, echoing the opinion of most of the players there that afternoon.

And for four decades since then historians have uncritically reinforced the myth. Microfilm of 17 sportswriters in attendance, representing 12 major papers reported something that didn't happen. The contradictory accounts of what eyewitnesses saw, or thought they saw, provide a fascinating study of the psychology of perception.

The proof in *l'affaire* Pesky is there for anyone to see. An unblinking, objective movie camera recorded the play. If Pesky held the ball, the camera would have seen it. But the film shows no such thing. So convincing is the cinematic record that Pesky and I will lay a wager with anyone who dares to take it: If you can look at the film of that play and are still convinced that Pesky did indeed hold the ball, we will buy you a steak dinner for two.

Has Pesky seen the film? "Hundreds of times," he sighs. Admittedly, the film is not comparable to today's instant-replay television tapes. It was shot in black and white from the shadows of the lower stands, behind home plate, without a zoom. We see Slaughter break from first base. We see Harry Walker slice a hit into center. We see Pesky dash into short left-center to take the relay. We see him catch Leon Culberson's throw, turn, and throw home, as Slaughter slides across the plate with room to spare. We can't see the details as clearly as we would like to, but there is no mistaking that Pesky caught, turned, and pegged, all in one motion.

"They say I dropped my arms," Pesky says. "I didn't drop my arms."

Poor Pesky. He has carried this cross for more than 40 years. If it had happened in 1986, or even, say, 1956, when television closeups and instant replays began to come into use, the tale could never have gotten started. We all know that Bill Buckner booted Mookie Wilson's ground ball in the 1986 Series. Millions of us saw it—and re-saw it and re-saw it.

But nobody saw Pesky hold the ball. They couldn't have, because he didn't.

Instead of playing the Series' seventh game on the Monday following the sixth game, both the Reds and the Cards took a day off, and the Cards sold tickets for Tuesday, October 15. So I heard one of the greatest games of the 20th century over the radio, listening to the lugubrious bass voice of Washington's Arch McDonald.

The Red Sox scored first against right-hander Murray Dickson (15-6). Wally Moses (.206) singled, and Pesky singled him to scoring position at third. Now Dom DiMaggio stood in like a bespectacled version of his brother Joe ("He's better than his brother Joe—Dominic DiMaggio"). I pictured him as "the Little Professor," looking donnish behind his thick goggles, and tugging alternately at his uniform shoulders in a characteristic mannerism. Dom had not had a good Series, hitting only .250 so far; he hadn't driven in a run. He lifted a fly to left to score Moses. Give Pesky an assist on the run. In the home half of the first, Red Schoendienst hit to left, and Williams made a good throw to Pesky, who made another good play to put the tag on the sliding Red and stopped that threat.

The Cardinals did score in the second against big, asthmatic Dave "Boo" Ferriss (25-6). Kurowski doubled and scored on a line drive to left by Harry "The Hat" Walker (.237). They went ahead in the fifth on Walker's single past Pesky, a sacrifice, and a double by Dickson (.277). Schoendienst singled through the box, and again Pesky made a good play, going to his left to smother the ball and prevent a run. But Terry Moore (.263) singled to make it 3-1. Sox manager Joe Cronin then called in Joe "Burrhead" Dobson (13-7) to pitch to Musial and Kurowski. Dobson threw his "atom ball" and got both on grounders.

In the eighth, the Sox were down to their last six outs. Russell pinch-hit another single, lefty George "Catfish" Metkovich (.246) doubled, sending Russell to third. Now Dyer called in Brecheen, who had had a day's rest, thanks to the off-day Monday. He got Moses to strike out, and Pesky lined to right.

DiMaggio was Boston's last hope. He lashed a long drive to the right-center field wall, as both runners scored to tie it up. "I knew the ball was between the outfielders," Dom, now a wealthy New England businessman, told me many years later. "I figured if I could get to third, it would make it a hell of a lot more difficult for Brecheen to pitch to Ted Williams. He might have made a wild pitch. So I tried to dig for a little extra." Dom's hustle probably cost Boston the championship, for he pulled a muscle in his leg as he tore around first and barely made it, limping painfully, into second. Dom had to be helped off the field, as Culberson, another wartime hold-over, trotted out to run for him. Williams tipped a foul back to Garagiola, breaking his finger and forcing him out of the game, too. Then Williams popped to second to end the inning.

Cronin looked to his bullpen. Would he bring in his ace, Hughson, who, like Brecheen, had had a day's rest? Or Johnson, who had slammed the door on the Cards back in game one? Cronin decided on Bob Klinger, a 38-year-old right-handed sinker baller with a record of 3-2 and 2.37. In those days relievers were not the stars they are now; the bullpen carried a stigma, where second-stringers, not good enough to start, were banished. Klinger had nine saves, a modest amount today but good enough to lead the league back then.

The first batter, Slaughter, playing with an injured arm, singled to center. Kurowski was next up. Kurowski tried to bunt but popped up. "My contribution has never been fully appreciated," he says today, smiling. Del Rice (.273), playing for Garagiola, flied to Culberson in center. Two outs.

That brought up Harry Walker. "If I had sacrificed," Kurowski says, "they would have walked Walker and pitched to the next guy," Marion (.233). Walker had been a bust in the '43 Series (.167) and had hit only .237 in the regular season in '46. However, he had been hot in the Series, hitting .375 so far (6-for-16). The following year he would lead the league with .363. He represented the Cardinals' last hope, for behind him were right-handed Marion and the pitcher. A spray hitter, Walker had already gotten one hit down the left field line, two to left-center, and two to right-center. The count went to 2-1. In the Sox dugout, DiMaggio says, he hobbled to the top of the steps and tried to wave Culberson over to the left, as Klinger wound up and pitched.

"Slaughter had a hell of a jump," Pesky says, "maybe six to eight steps." Pesky moved toward the bag for a possible play there, and Walker swung.

Walker says he didn't try to place the ball but simply hit it where it was pitched, to left-center. Culberson in straight-away center wasn't out of position, Walker says; if Culberson had been too far to the left, he risked letting a ball get by him to the right, which might have been a triple. Most newspaper reports say the ball was a looping Texas-leaguer. Cronin remembered that it took "a funny hop." Walker disagrees. It "scooted" on the hard St. Louis grass almost to the wall at the 375-foot mark, he says.

It was to Culberson's glove-hand side; Williams would have been in a poor position to throw. Culberson, who played deeper than DiMaggio, got to it first "in rather remote left-center field," according to Burt Whitman of the Boston *Herald*. Culberson fielded it across his body and heaved it homeward while Slaughter, who had already torn around second, roared full speed toward third.

Here the eye-witnesses disagree. Culberson fielded it "with neatness and dispatch," reported J. Roy Stockton of the St. Louis *Post Dispatch*, and "made a quick relay," says Jack Hand of the AP. But Shirley Povich of the Washington *Post* thought that Culberson's throw was "an unforgivably lazy lob, and perhaps it was that throw which lulled Pesky into a false sense of sureness that Slaughter would hold up at third."

Another part of the myth is that Cardinal third-base coach Mike Gonzalez was frantically signaling Slaughter to stop. He had been criticized in Boston for sending two runners home and both were gunned down. Was he playing it safe this time? In later years Slaughter said he ran right through Gonzalez's red light.

Hell no, Gonzalez insisted later. With the bottom of the batting order up next, he was down the line waving his arms like a windmill, urging Slaughter to keep going: "I say, 'Go on, go on!' and he go."

Hand says Gonzalez "flapped the come-on sign like an excited mother hen." That's what Stockton, Povich, and Gus Steiger of the New York

Daily Mirror also saw, though Steiger admitted he thought Gonzalez "was sending Slaughter to almost certain death." Of the 17 writers studied, no others mentioned the coach at all.

But Slaughter admitted in the locker room later: "Yeah, Mike told me to keep going."

Would Slaughter have tried it with DiMaggio in the outfield? "No," he says flatly. "I've said that many times. You know DiMaggio had a great arm, but Culberson didn't have too good of an arm, and he wasn't as quick as DiMaggio. DiMaggio would have gotten rid of it a lot quicker. I don't think I would have even tried."

Dom DiMaggio himself is convinced that he not only would have had a good shot at Slaughter at the plate: "He might not even have tried to go to third."

Pesky said later that Culberson bobbled the ball momentarily. Walker denies it. "Culberson didn't bobble the ball, and he didn't throw it bad. It was a perfect throw to Pesky." Maybe DiMaggio would have been a few steps faster, Walker shrugs, but even DiMaggio couldn't have thrown Slaughter out on the fly from deep left-center.

Pesky, meanwhile, had reversed direction, dashing into the outfield grass to take Culberson's throw. His back was toward home, and he didn't see Slaughter at all.

"Williams and I yelled to him," Culberson says: "Home! Home!" Doerr, covering second as Walker steamed around first, also yelled, and he was only 100 feet from Pesky. But 36,143 St. Louis fans were also screaming. "Everyone was screaming and hollering," Pesky says, "and the place was full."

"I didn't hear anything either," Walker agrees.

Walker says he decided to stretch his hit deliberately in order to draw a throw from Pesky, or at least make Pesky turn to his right for a possible play there. "I was watching Slaughter make the turn at third," Walker says. "Because I came into second—that's what made Pesky look. The whole play balanced around that. He probably would have thrown him out if he'd gone the other way." Doerr also says Pesky turned "just enough to take a peek."

Of 15 reporters who say they saw Pesky hesitate, only two, Hand and Irving Vaughan of the Chicago *Tribune*, reported seeing Pesky turn toward Walker. If they all had their eyes glued to Pesky, as they claim, why did only two see him pivot the wrong way?

"A lot of people say I turned to the right," Pesky says, "but I didn't."

The camera agrees with him; it clearly shows him turning to his left to throw.

Vaughan added another detail that no other reporter remarked on. Slaughter had reached third, he wrote, detected Pesky looking the wrong way, then "broke for the plate." Everyone else agrees that Slaughter did not stop to look at Pesky but was charging full-tilt around third, his eyes on the plate.

Slaughter raced into the shadows cast by the late autumn sun. Cronin, a Hall-of-Fame shortstop himself, said it took Pesky a split-second to focus his eyes and pick up Slaughter. "I wanted to make sure I had the ball," Pesky says. "There was a smoky haze over the ballpark, but I picked him up right away."

At this moment, Hand wrote, Pesky "dropped his arm halfway," before he realized Slaughter was hot-footing it home. Did Johnny hesitate, or drop his arms, for the fateful split second?

"No," says John emphatically. "I wanted to get rid of the ball as fast as I could."

The camera agrees with Pesky and not with the writers. The film shows one continuous movement—catch, wheel, throw.

How did he throw?

Again, the witnesses don't agree. Whitman wrote that Pesky threw "too late and too weakly." But Harold Kease of the rival Boston *Globe* said Pesky "sent the ball whistling toward the plate." Povich called it "a rifle throw."

"When I picked Slaughter up," Pesky remembers, "he was maybe 20-30 feet from home plate. He must have sprung wings. I would have had to have a cannon for an arm." His throw was up the line. It wasn't even close.

Even if everything had gone perfectly, Doerr says, "there's a question in my mind whether he would have caught Slaughter."

Far from choking, the Red Sox almost tied it up in their ninth. York and Doerr (.409 for the Series) led off with two quick singles, and Higgins' fielder's choice put the tying run on third with one out. But Partee fouled to Musial, and McBride, the hero of the first game, hit a bounder to second base. The Series was over. And Pesky was the goat.

Most, though not all, of the papers the next day blamed Pesky for holding the ball. A few writers ignored the play or down-played it. But the consensus of the writers stands in contrast to the stark record of what the camera saw.

After studying the conflicting evidence, I've concluded the following:

The play happened fast, about nine seconds from Walker's bat meeting the ball to Slaughter's slide across home. Up in the press box, the writers had to watch the ball while squinting into the sun, and Slaughter racing into the shadows, Culberson's throw and Pesky's relay—an impossible feat for anyone with less than eight eyes. Those who were watching the ball could not simultaneously have been watching Slaughter, and vice versa.

Here let us flashback six years to the seventh game of the 1940 World Series, the Tigers against the Reds. Detroit was leading 1-0 in the last of the seventh, which Cincinnati's Frank McCormick opened with a double. Jimmy Ripple also drove a long one into the outfield, and Detroit shortstop Dick Bartell turned to take the relay. With his back to the plate and with the Cincinnati fans in a frenzy, Bartell was unaware that the lumbering McCormick was trying to score. He held the ball just long enough to let McCormick across the plate with the tying run. Ripple scored the winner a few moments later on a long fly.

Bartell's fatal pause was still in the memory of many of the reporters in St. Louis in 1946. Perhaps someone in the press box, possibly Hand, who was the most emphatic in his report the next morning, yelled out, "Did you see that? Did you see that? Pesky held the ball!" Most of the writers had probably been watching Slaughter, not Pesky. But none of them wanted to be accused by their editors back home of missing the Key Play of the Series. So they sheepishly but dutifully wrote that Pesky held the ball.

Of the 17 newspaper accounts studied, 15 said he did. Two—Joe Trimble of the New York *Daily News* and Martin J. Haley of the St. Louis *Globe Democrat*—didn't mention it at all in their stories.

Many of the others placed the incident low in their reports. Steiger put it in paragraph 14 on the jump page. Rud Rennie of the New York *Herald Tribune* had it in paragraph seven. If it had been such a key play, as everyone today believes it was, why didn't these seasoned reporters put it in their leads?

Some fudged. Bob Burnes, sports editor for the *Globe Democrat*, wrote that Slaughter scored "while the Red Sox stood and watched." That was safe—some 36,000 people were all standing and watching.

John Drebinger of the *Times* merely said Pesky was "bewildered," which implies that Drebinger was reading Pesky's mind but does not describe what Pesky actually did.

Red Smith of the *Herald Tribune* had the most colorful description of all: Pesky "stood morosely studying Ford Frick's signature on the ball. . . .

At length, he turned dreamily, gave a small start of astonishment . . . and threw in sudden panic." Red's prose shows why he won so many prizes as a great stylist, but it is of no use as reportage.

It's a pity we do not have a tape recording of what broadcaster Arch McDonald saw. That would give us a spontaneous reaction to the play, uncolored by what anyone else, in another part of the press box, may have said then or later.

Meanwhile, without a TV replay to dispute it, a myth was born.

The myth has served Slaughter well. With that historic dash, he raced all the way into the Hall of Fame—it is questionable whether he would be there now without it. Slaughter would embellish it with the secondary myth that he had disobeyed Gonzalez's signal in order to seize the championship, a myth that Gonzalez himself tried to deny, but no one would listen. After all, what did Slaughter do? He got a good jump and scored from first on a double. It's a routine play that one sees hundreds of times every season. (In later years the official scorer's decision, a double, was changed to a single, then changed back to the original double.)

The myth was also good for Walker's ego. His story of faking Pesky out makes a good hot-stove tale.

Above all, the myth has served, for over 40 years, to protect the real goat of the Series by deflecting blame onto the innocent Pesky. For who else was the goat except Klinger, who gave up the single and double which lost the game? Klinger died in 1977 without coming to Pesky's defense or offering to take the goat horns on his own forehead.

Second guessers also wondered why Cronin had used Klinger instead of Hughson, who was just as well rested as Brecheen. Or why Cronin hadn't switched to a left-hander, Johnson, or Mickey Harris (17-9) with the left-handers Slaughter and Walker coming up? Cronin never did reply.

"It was one of those things," says Pesky. "What are you going to do? Things have happened to better ballplayers than me. They're looking for the good guy and the bad guy. Some people want to blame me, but that's OK,"—he smiles wanly—"as long as they don't get physical. Baseball is a game of mistakes, and you make one, you're going to hear about it. I've been called a bum many times. But deep down in my own heart, I know I didn't do anything wrong."

OUR FRIEND WILLIE

Bill Klink

OUR MEMORIES OF HIM at the Polo Grounds, Seals Stadium, Candlestick Park, and finally Shea Stadium don't seem to fade. Willie Mays, the "Say-hey Kid," "Leo's Favorite." All the great throws, the Wertz catch, the dramatic home run to move the Giants into a 1962 playoff with the Dodgers . . . we remember them all.

But what was he like before he got to New York and started hitting home runs and playing stickball in the streets? What about his first three months as a professional in Trenton, New Jersey—three months which propelled him to Minneapolis for six weeks in 1951, then on to the Giants?

Mays' Trenton teammates have lent us their memories to weave the story of a shy, almost reticent, player, who emerged not only as a team player—amazing all with eye-popping catches and throws—but who also broke the color barrier in a league whose boundaries stretched into the South.

The 1950 Trenton Giants were a lackluster team mired in fourth place, just two games over .500 and seven games behind league-leading Hagerstown, when Willie Mays was assigned to the team in New Jersey's capitol city. Until then, its only motto was, "Trenton makes, the world takes." The club's slow start that year was a disappointment to Giants fans and to its new manager, "Chick" Genovese, who inherited only Mo Cunningham and two spot starters from the pitching staff from the 1949 championship team. Genovese and the Trenton Giants needed Willie, just as the New York Giants and Leo Durocher would need him less than a year later in May 1951, when the New Yorkers "went through a nine game losing streak and the ball club looked like anything but a pennant winner," according to

Roger Bowman, formerly a kingpin on the 1947 Trenton championship team and a reliever on the '51 Miracle Giants.

Mays almost didn't have the chance to perform miracles with the 1950 Trenton team. He switched trains from Washington, D.C. to Hagerstown on his journey from his home in Birmingham to join the team. As a result, Bill McKechnie, Trenton's business manager, and the rest of the official welcoming committee came up short a center fielder and started to leave the railway station without Mays. A railroad patrolman spotted Mays atop his two suitcases adjacent to the station and McKechnie hustled his new find off to the ballpark.

On the eve of his pro debut, there was some question as to whether Mays would make his mark as an outfielder. The scouting report on Mays' three-quarters-overhand throwing motion said that with such an arm, if he slumped at the plate from the outset, Mays would have ably filled the Giants' pitching needs. Ironically, though he later briefly played several infield positions as well as the outfield with the San Francisco Giants, he would never be asked to pitch. The night of June 24, 1950, Mays walked into the Hagerstown, Maryland stadium and became the first black to play in the Interstate League.

Herb Boetto, the Trenton catcher, recalled that first game. "The night he came to Hagerstown the papers had a big headline, 'Giants sign black player; Will be playing in game tonight.' Bill McKechnie, Jr., the general manager, and Willie were late getting there and the game had already started. The clubhouse was on the right field foul line and we had a capacity crowd that night. I remember McKechnie drove him up and we were in the third base side dugout. He suited him up down the right field line and, as Willie jogged all the way around, the entire stands booed. It was really something. But he was really good and didn't say anything.

"I can remember one comment he made after he hit for the first time. He said, 'Me and that guy are going to get along real good before the game's over with,' meaning the pitcher . . . because he could hit him."

Eric Rodin, the team's right fielder and now a successful building contractor in Flemington, New Jersey, concurs. "As far as hitting was concerned, Willie learned a little bit. The pitchers took advantage. They shook him up a little but Willie never said anything. They'd knock him down and he'd just stare at 'em. But get out of the way 'cause he was going to rip one on the next pitch!"

Len Matte, Trenton's other catcher, recalls that the Giants took up the slack when things got out of hand and Mays was nonplussed. "There were racial slurs thrown out which we were taking and, frankly, things got to a heated point. We always told Willie, 'We'll take care of this,' and he never got involved. He was there to play ball. All he wanted to know was, 'What time do we start and what time do we finish?'"

First night jitters behind him, Mays quickly emerged as the consummate ballplayer, hitting .353 while gathering 108 hits (but only four home runs) in just 81 games. The Trenton Giants went 46-36-3 with Mays in center field the last ten weeks of the season. Although they lost the five-game championship series to Hagerstown's Braves four games to one, Mays got seven hits, including two doubles and four triples, with four RBIs. He was barely nosed out by Danny Schell of Wilmington (and later, the Phillies) for league MVP. Willie gained six first-place votes to Schell's five, but the Blue Hens' outfielder had four more second-place tallies than Willie.

Mays was forced to room by himself due to Jim Crow laws in a number of cities, and surely felt apart. But when he was with the club, even as the youngest member of a veteran team in a "fast" Class-B league, Willie fit in easily. Boetto remembers: "The thing about Willie was that he was loose. We'd be on the team bus and it would surprise me, he'd just start talking—just talk—he was crazy! The guys got such a kick out of Willie. Never at any point did we feel like he was anything but a team member, even though he couldn't stay at some of the hotels we stayed at—even in Trenton."

Mays' ability to seemingly always enjoy the game that first year, in spite of the hardships of being the league's first black player, is well illustrated in an analogy Rodin makes. "I think it was like most of us when we'd get an electric train for Christmas. Playing baseball was Willie's electric train. He never cried about the heat, the hardships; never said anything about having to room in Hagerstown over in the black district, or about not being able to stay at the Rodney Hotel in Wilmington.

"His attitude towards us in terms of kidding around made the days very enjoyable, instead of being a drudgery to play. He was a kid; it was like having apple pie, ice cream, and cake for him just to be on the baseball field. That was the way he participated in the game, and never had an ulcer in his life from any racial incidents that might have happened."

Mays and diminutive manager Chick Genovese enjoyed a special relationship. A fielding star on three pennant-winning Louisville Colonels teams in the 1940s, Genovese played in 269 consecutive games without an error, but still never cracked the majors. He was a respected and valued member of those Colonel teams. At the tail end of World War II, Louisville officials had a lifesize poster of Chick placed in front of the factories where they wanted people to be efficient, according to his brother, George, a long-time Giants scout. The poster read, "He's efficient at his job—you be efficient at yours!"

It was just that type of efficiency Genovese was trying to instill in Mays when he helped develop (or streamline, depending on the source of the story) the basket, or 'soft,' catch as Genovese preferred to call it.

Len Matte, who now owns an insurance agency in Hamilton Square, New Jersey, is more forceful. "I don't know if Willie's ever given credit to anybody for his basket catch, but I was there. I worked with Willie and Chick on it. The first night he came to Hagerstown, Chick had me out there with him, and Chick was hitting balls to him long distance. He was going all kinds of ways—from one end of the field to the other. Chick said to me, 'This guy has the kind of reflexes no one else has.' Willie proved that later on in the year by knowing where to go without even looking at the ball. I think the catch in the World Series of 1954 proved that."

Matte continues, "Anyhow, Chick took him aside right away and told him, 'Willie, you're going to make an awful lot of money someday and I'm going to help you make it.' Chick told Willie, 'You have to do something different than anybody else,' and that's how the basket catch was developed."

Bell adds, "I saw where Durocher or somebody supposedly taught it to him, but that wasn't true. I remember Chick teaching him that. I can vividly remember Genovese teaching him that."

Some saw the relationship as more one-dimensional—a case of the minor-league manager riding the coattails of the star on the rise. Joe "Jeep" Micciche, now owner of a dress manufacturing firm on Staten Island, recalls, "Chick really idolized the man. He went really gung-ho for Willie. Like any minor-league ballplayer, the manager is hungry, too. The manager wants to win so he can also advance. If he produced good ballplayers for the organization, and they saw it, they'd advance him. So when Chick had something good, he'd ride him to the hilt."

Bell, the second baseman, agrees. "Chick was like a cheerleader when Willie was up there—a little bantam rooster down there at third base waving Willie on."

Eric Rodin, a cocky right fielder who was viewed by many as having the best right arm in the league until Mays' arrival, sees it differently: "Genovese was probably one of the best fielding outfielders in organized baseball during his years of playing. Chick was very patient with most of us in his own way. As far as teaching Mays anything—the basket was Willie's way of playing. He did try to help him in some ways to help *improve* his fielding.

"Mays was an individual who really didn't need tutoring. As a matter of fact, I'd probably have asked him to help tutor me. He just had that unique ability which most people do not have, so I really don't think that Chick helped him on that end. But I think what Chick did was the beginning of what Leo Durocher did with our friend Willie. He tried to be a guardian angel or father to him at that point and to guide him."

Other players sensed something special between the two. Bobby Myers, the team's first baseman, now baseball coach at Long Beach City College, recalls, "Mays had a tremendous feeling for our manager, Genovese—I can't say he really idolized him—but I think Chick knew right away what he had. I don't know what direction Chick had from Jack Schwarz (Giants' Director of Scouting) or Hubbell up in New York, and while he didn't take Willie under his wing in the same way, I can't believe that Durocher showed him any more compassion and feeling than Genovese did. Chick was just a tremendous influence on him, because Willie did struggle a little bit the first three or four games and then he went crazy!"

A manager's special touch wasn't the only reason the Giants placed Mays in a previously segregated B league, according to Ed Monahan, pitching ace of the team and now a Vice-President with Equitable Life in New York. "I think the biggest reason they chose Trenton was that it was near New York. Stoneham and the group could come down, which they did several times. We had a decent team and they realized that, along with the fact that (general manager Bill) McKechnie was a pretty intelligent guy, Chick was good with young players so they figured that Trenton was the way to go. Trenton, for Willie's ability, was a good league—plus it was close to New York. Stoneham stopped in for three or four games, which was extraordinary."

Photographs have forever etched in our memory the catch and throw Willie Mays made in the eighth inning of Game One of the 1954 World Series. Class B ball being what it was in 1950, no such photographs exist of two of the finer catches Mays ever made. Those catches, however, did make a lasting impression on the players who witnessed them in the summer of 1950.

The first was in tiny Dunn Field in Trenton, in the third inning of Willie's first game before the home fans on June 27. Rodin was closest to Mays and observed: "Mays played center field, I was playing right field, and Cunningham was in left at the old Trenton park called Dunn Field. We had a center field there that was 405 feet from home plate. The batter, Bill Biddle, hit a line shot—I guess it was about the second inning—to dead center. It was carrying toward the center field fence and probably would have gone over it. I can remember coming over to take the play off the fence, assuming that Mays would not catch it. The amazing thing about what happened was that Mays went up with his gloved hand to catch the ball and at that moment the ball had passed the glove. But his reflexes were such that he went up with his bare hand against the fence, caught the ball bare-handed and came down."

As it would four years later with the fabled Wertz catch, Mays' throw put the icing on the cake. Boetto finishes the play:

"The grass that night in Trenton, as it always was, was moist and the ball had such velocity on it that it took off and then caught me in the throat and knocked me cold. He made such a play from the outfield that the guy from third couldn't score on a ball that was hit over Willie's head!"

Mays, growing more confident with every game he played, was unmoved. Pitcher Jim Arbucho, now a businessman in Englewood, New York, recalls, "When he got into the dugout, I said to him, 'Hey, you mean you caught that ball bare-handed?' Willie said nonchalantly, 'Yeah, I couldn't get my glove hand up in time so I caught it bare-handed.' Man, what a play!"

Matte, like many of this Trenton team, didn't know how to react. "Everybody, including us, didn't know what to say. It's like this guy dropped out of the sky from somewhere!"

York, Pennsylvania's Memorial Stadium in the Interstate League may not have been as spacious as the Polo Grounds, but it was the scene for Mays' second fielding gem of the year, on July 23. York's White Roses had loaded the bases with two outs in the fifth of a 1-1 ballgame. Bill Biddle (again) was the victim.

Cunningham was closest to the action this time in left field. "Biddle really hit a ball to left center. Mays ran into a low wire fence at the base of an incline and took the ball just as he hit the fence and did a somersault over the fence and held the ball. It was just a matter of whether he was going to hold it when he started going over the fence."

Arbucho puts the situation in perspective. "When you turned around and all you saw was a man's numbers on his back, you knew he had a good jump on the ball. If you saw him staring at you, you knew you better back up third base! But if you see his numbers, he's got a jump on that ball and he has a good shot to catch it. With Willie, to my recollection, anytime I turned around, all I saw were numbers."

With only four home runs to his credit for the year, Mays wasn't going to earn a promotion for his power hitting. At 168 pounds, he was not yet the power hitter he would become in New York.

Heitschmidt, now a trainmaster with the Grand Trunk Railroad in Kalamazoo, Michigan, says: "Willie hit a lot of what ballplayers call 'frozen ropes.' He was a natural hitter. I don't think he ran across anyone in our league that year who was too quick for him—that he couldn't get that bat around on. But he was primarily a spray hitter when he came with Trenton and he hit the line drives."

Mays became lethal, Heitschmidt recalls, when Genovese was able to call pitches (fast ball, off-speed pitch) from his third base coaching box by the third inning. "Willie was a good enough hitter that you didn't have to call pitches for him, but on occasions when Chick would, Willie attacked the ball. He looked like a pinball machine."

Myers remembers a slightly different Mays in terms of his physical strength. "It's interesting, he had the biggest forearms I've ever seen in my life. I'm not the biggest guy in the world but I'd like to think I was fairly strong. Well, Willie and I were fooling around one day—just arm wrestling, and he took me down with no problem whatsoever. He had a fantastic upper half of his body, just unbelievably strong. Talk about 'Popeye forearms'—he had 'em, just tremendously strong."

His fielding and hitting an important commodity in the Trenton Giants pennant drive, Mays was asked to play every day without rest. While this was not an uncommon occurrence in the Interstate League, it was hard on Mays, who played every game as though it were his last. From June 24 to August 28, he did not miss a game. Trenton had played *five* consecutive doubleheaders from August 23 to the 27th. But during the first game of the August 28 doubleheader, disaster struck.

Boetto remembers: "Throughout his career, Mays would have a fainting spell towards the end of the season. Coming off the field, he did this in Harrisburg, Pennsylvania. We had played something like six doubleheaders and I caught most of them. I was as tired as anyone, and I can recall after the third or fourth one, Willie coming off the field, stumbling, and falling to the ground. Gosh, they called an ambulance. He did this years later, on occasion, towards the end of the year—he'd have this breakdown. I used to laugh about it because he used to do this when he was with us."

For most of the 1950 Trenton Giants, those brief weeks teamed up with Willie Mays were the most memorable of their lives. Many continued to see Mays as he toured the National League parks through the 1950s and '60s and enjoyed much the same "special relationship" with him that the late Chick Genovese did.

Jim Arbucho, the tall pitcher who retired late in the season, sums up the feelings of this group of players. "At Trenton, Willie was just small in stature. All of a sudden he grew—from a bulb into a flower—you know what I mean?"

VEECK
AND THE MIDGET

Bob Broeg

BILL VEECK, a self-styled bleacher bum, wore no man's collar, not even his own. He was the game's greatest iconoclast, a turncoat to other club-owners even though he wore no coat on the coldest days. He was, indeed, the Barnum of Baseball and deserves to be remembered for many things. But, indubitably, he will be remembered best for the day he played a midget!

Veeck still had almost half his hard, fast 71 years left after he titillated a crowd and horrified traditionalists by slipping midget Eddie Gaedel into the batter's box on Sunday, August 19, 1951. At 26 years old, Gaedel was the right age, but the wrong size to be a big-league ballplayer. He stood only 3'7" and weighed just 65 pounds.

I'm thankful not only to have seen and covered the occasion but also for being tipped off beforehand. Otherwise, a famous photograph would not have been taken to prove that, honest Injun, the midget was not merely a figment of your imagination.

The whole story actually has an O. Henry twist. Permit me to set the stage with the cast of characters—and I emphasize "characters"—who perpetrated baseball's grandest hoax.

It was right down Bill Veeck's fun-loving alley. An inveterate fan at best and a baseball broker at worst, he grew up in a ballpark or, at least, the neighborhood firehouse behind the left field wall at Wrigley Field. His father was general manager of the Cubs and Bill hustled soda in the stands, reveling at his heroes' pennant success in 1929, '32 and '35.

Too liberal for even a liberal college, Kenyon, Veeck returned to the Cubs, draped the traditional ivy on the brick outfield walls at the ballpark and became a young (age 27) treasurer. But he was a disrespectful maverick even then. So Phil Wrigley canned him in 1941. Veeck teamed with an old friend and idol, former first baseman/manager Charley Grimm, and bought the minor-league Milwaukee Brewers.

His foot was crushed by a faulty recoil of an anti-aircraft gun when Veeck was a World War II Marine in the South Pacific. Divorced from a circus bareback rider, he was undaunted. Bill played winning tennis with an artificial leg, until he lost so much of the leg that he adopted a Long-John-Silver wooden peg, conveniently storing tabs of the six-packs of cigarrettes he smoked in it. Meanwhile, he began his big-league hocus-pocus as a bone in American League clubowners' throats.

Backed by a loyal consortium, he bought the Cleveland Indians in 1946 and, mixing his win-*or*-have-fun philosophy, he dazzled the Indians with his clever promotions and bold moves. He dipped into the black leagues for the American League's first black player (Larry Doby) and then hired an aging legend (Satchel Paige), who helped the ball club to a 1948 world championship and 2,620,627 attendance—still formidable, then stunning.

By then, I'd often go from a late-night session with Bill directly to an early-morning stint on the copy desk, my eyes burning from lack of sleep. But you never worried about sleep when you were around Bill. He was a great host and most charming company. He was a tireless dynamo. Tugging at his dwindling curls and wrinkling his corrugated forehead in agitation, he discussed and argued politics and baseball, played musical-comedy records and told interesting tales.

For instance, in 1938 when, after a night on the town with Bunny Berrigan in Chicago, he had poured hot, black coffee into the reeling horn player and half-carried Berrigan into a recording studio. There, half-stiffed, Berrigan played and sang his classic "Can't Get Started With You."

Veeck, after buying the Browns in 1951 from the brothers DeWitt, Bill and Charley, soon turned the club's former ballpark offices into an apartment for him, for lovely second wife Mary Frances and their first son, Mike. Shortly after all of us left, just before the cock crowed, Bill would sink into a steaming-hot tub of bath water to soothe searing nerve ends of the retreating, war-wounded leg.

At times he would catnap, but, usually, he read books voraciously. Before and after illness forced him out of baseball, the first time in 1961 and then in 1980 with spiraling salary costs because of free agency and inflation, he read for fun and for knowledge. He reviewed books for newspapers and also provided service as a paid lecturer.

But back when he took over the Brownies, he'd be out bright and breakfast-early, hustling his team like a service-club speaker. One morning, as often, broadcaster Bud Blattner picked him up. A young, former big-league infielder, Blattner burned the midnight oil with Veeck and drank it. This time, en route to a meeting, Bill lamented the lack of a little lead off man, noting how often the champion Yankees' 5'6" shortstop, Phil Rizzuto, reached base and—

"Suddenly," says Blattner, "Bill turned to me and I could see that look in his eyes—like a pinball machine on tilt."

Veeck called in his public relations man, Bob Fishel, ultimately executive Vice-President of the American League. Typically, Fishel fit the image of the talent lured by the Pied Piper of Baseball. Fishel, an ex-serviceman, was an Indians' fan working in advertising in Cleveland when Bill came to town. Veeck located him by telephone in the office of Paul Brown, the first coach of the Cleveland Browns football team.

It was love at first conversation. Fishel went to work with Veeck in Cleveland, then moved to St. Louis with him. Robert O. Fishel— "Roberto," as Veeck called him—grinned when the smiling owner unveiled his devilish plan. Sure, why not? "Besides," said Fishel, "if Bill had his mind made up, you couldn't change it anyway."

So Veeck phoned a former Cleveland actor's agent, Marty Caine, then in Chicago. He wanted a midget, not a dwarf, but a midget, a *special* midget. Secrecy was paramount. Caine sent in several midgets, most of them from St. Louis. Veeck rejected them. They were too old. Too ugly. Too tall.

Finally, from Chicago, where the midget did bits for an ad company, came the one Veeck wanted.

In a word, Eddie Gaedel was cute.

When Bill gave thumbs-up to the half-pint, Fishel drove Eddie south from the ballpark on Grand Avenue to a point near a handsome movie house, the Fox. There, seated in Bob's Packard, Eddie signed three American League contracts.

Fishel remembers, smiling: "We offered $100 and expenses." Gaedel flew back to Chicago, expected back the day that would mark St. Louis's celebration of the American League's 50th anniversary. Veeck mailed a copy of Edwin F. Gaedel's contract, too late to reach League offices in Chicago before Monday.

Over the years, Veeck loved doing the unexpected. Oh, sure, now and then he would announce a giveaway of an orchid to each woman who attended, but, preferably, he liked surprises, even big ones, like a spanking new automobile. He would have a crate of cackling chickens delivered to a "lucky" fan or have a 100-pound cake of ice deposited at a customer's seat on a hot night. Or if he was going to provide a can of fruit or vegetables to all, he would have the wrappers removed. If you loved peaches, you might end up with a can of peas.

The night before baseball history was rewritten, my wife and I were among a few lounging with Veeck, sipping beer, listening to music and playing charades, a game at which Veeck was an enthusiastic master. He later rendezvoused with me in the john.

Aware that the last newspaper edition had already gone to bed, he told me slyly about the pint-sized *piece de resistance* at tomorrow's doubleheader with Detroit.

He expectantly waited when he delivered the punchline. I laughed.

He was pleased, but, hell, as Fishel had said, I don't think it would make any difference.

Still, his tip-off was significant: when *Post-Dispatch* photographer Jack January showed up Sunday, aware that often a short-staffed crew might cut out, I urged him to stay. At a time when photographers were permitted on the playing field, he would line up as close as possible.

One other person had to know—the Browns' manager, of course. James Wren "Zack" Taylor, a grizzled 53-year-old, knew the rules of employment. He had lasted 16 years in the majors as a smart second-string catcher. He "stayed out of the double play," that is, repeatedly hit ground balls to the right side. As a coach when the Browns had a one-armed outfielder in 1945, Taylor was a picture-book loyalist. For Veeck, he would later let the fans help him "grandstand manage" in another orchestration. He also would have to permit Satchel Paige to sit in an old-fashioned rocking chair. So, heck, give me a copy of the contract, boss.

When Gaedel flew into town Sunday morning, he was cabbed to Veeck's apartment. There, Bill produced a miniature Browns' uniform, worn by the young son of the former club owner. The midget was given a couple of toy bats. Friskily, he swung one. Veeck halted him.

"Hold it, kid," Veeck said. "I'm going on the roof to direct the show between games. If you so much as swing at a pitch, I'll shoot you—and I was an expert rifleman in the Marines."

Gaedel nodded.

He was slipped down to the empty clubhouse used by the Cardinals, then tenants of the Browns. He listened to the first game of the double-header—lost, as usual. Between games, manager Taylor visted Gaedel. The midget's confidence was wavering. It shook further when Taylor tied Gaedel's miniature baseball shoes and said, with a touch of truth as well as humor, "I think you'll be all right kid. I don't think they'll throw *at* you."

The nervous little kid jumped to his feet, ready to grab his fashionable little duds and head back to Chicago, but looming in the doorway was the Browns' traveling secretary.

"Listen, kid, if you don't do what you've been told and *when*, I'll pinch your head," said secretary Bill Durney, feigning anger, "and you heard Bill Veeck. He'll be on the rooftop with a high-powered rifle."

Veeck *was* on the rooftop, a Cecil B. DeMille of the Diamond with a bullhorn, directing anniversary intermission activities. Fans entering the park had been given an ice-cream bar and a piece of cake. Between games, salt-and-pepper shakers were distributed, as were copies of the American League's golden-anniversary souvenir booklet. From the rooftop, Veeck waved on an eight-piece roving band dressed in uniforms of the Naughty Nineties. Aerial bombs exploded, casting miniature flags to the field. Old-fashioned autos and cycles fringed the field in parade. A hand balancer performed at first base, trampoline artists tumbled at second, and a juggler juggled at third.

A four-piece band of Brownie players walked onto the middle of the field—Satchel Paige on the drums, Al Widmar with a bull-fiddle, Ed Redys with an accordion and Johnny Berardino maneuvered the moroccos.

Suddenly a giant papier-mache cake was wheeled onto the field. The band played "Happy Birthday" and up and out through the top layer popped a little guy with a fractional number on his back. Quickly, he ran off into the home team's third-base dugout. The crowd laughed happily. Wasn't that a clever climax?

Climax? Haw!

After Detroit failed to score in the first inning, a moral victory for the Browns, who were surging to a 52-102 cellar season, field announcer Bernie Ebert droned, "For the Browns, number 1/8, Eddie Gaedel, batting for Frank Saucier . . ."

I held my breath. The crowd gasped as the cute little man came out, vigorously swinging miniature bats. Would Ed Hurley, the hot-tempered Boston Irishman umpiring behind the plate, spoil the show?

Arms folded firmly across his chest, staring straight ahead, Hurley merely wiggled fingers of his right hand toward the third-base dugout. *Taylor, get your butt out here to home plate.* And here came Taylor loping out, tugging characteristically with one hand at his knee-length baseball bloomers and waving a copy of the contract in the other. Glancing at the contract, Hurley didn't flinch. He shrugged, motioned Gaedel to the plate and beckoned to the pitcher, Bob Cain, age 26, the same as the midget.

Meanwhile, hurrying out of the Detroit dugout came the Tigers' manager, Red Rolfe. Although tipped off shortly beforehand about Veeck's "secret weapon," Rolfe protested only mildly. After all, the Tigers were only a fifth-place ball club in 1951. (Rolfe would acknowledge to me later, "I think Bill went a bit too far. I don't blame him for wanting to entertain his fans, but I don't think anything should be permitted that might affect the game or make a joke out of it.")

At the time, the Tigers' bench gave Gaedel a rousing, growling welcome. "Get outta that hole, runt," they chorused. At the same time, too, the Detroit battery conferred. Catcher Bob Swift went out to Cain. The left-hander wondered if he could throw the ball underhanded—as in softball? No, the catcher told him, Hurley wouldn't permit that. Maybe, Swift suggested, he could go back and lie down behind the plate? No, this time the pitcher threw the cold water, the umpire really would get into a huff. Swift nodded and retreated behind the plate.

Small became smaller as the midget crouched. Cain could not get the ball low enough, lobbing it, and Gaedel dutifully did not swing. At Ball Four, Eddie triumphantly threw aside his bat and dashed to first base. Quickly, Jim Delsing, who would replace Saucier in right field and still is identified as "the man who ran for the midget," came out to replace Gaedel.

When Gaedel reached first, unhurt and finished, the weight seemed to leave his shoulders. Spiritually, he seemed to soar in relief as he gazed upward. When Delsing tagged the bag, the midget made a grand gesture, reaching up to pat the taller man on the fanny. Amid louder cheers, Eddie raced off the field into the Browns' dugout and, obviously, to the clubhouse directly behind it.

Rather than rush right down to the clubhouse, forgetting that Cain and Company would do what came naturally to the Browns (beat them 6-2), I remained a stationary press-box *dummkopp*. To Fishel, I wondered how long the midget would be around the park? When Roberto suggested he would be catching a plane shortly, I did a double-take and urged the P.R. man to bring him to the press box so I could talk with him.

Minutes later, here came the midget, his appearance and attire still fresh in my mind's eye. He word light tan slacks, a yellow sports shirt, neatly draped by a medium-dark sports coat. Neat.

When Fishel introduced us, I picked up the little man and sat him on the press-box tabletop, where his feet swung merrily. He said excitedly, "For a minute, I felt like Babe Ruth."

"You know Eddie, you little S.O.B., you're now what I always wanted to be?"

"What's that?" he asked.

"An ex-big-leaguer."

The significance of the day sank in. Gaedel straightened, puffed out his chest with obvious pride, smiled and leaped off the counter and stalked off with a cheery good-bye.

The story of the midget in an official big-league at bat amused many. Not, however, starchy Will Harridge, high-collared American League president who received, by telegram from Veeck, the "release" of Edwin F. Gaedel as a "player" the same day his signed contract arrived. Mr. Harridge immediately issued a scathing, never-let-it-happen-again edict and, huffily, he officially expunged Gaedel from the record books.

"H'mm," mused Veeck, "I wonder how they can balance Bob Cain's bases on balls? Actually, I wanted to prove this idea was practical. We almost scored a run that inning, filling the bases. I wish Mr. Harridge would tell me what the maximum and minimum heights are. If David hadn't been so small, who would remember his fight with Goliath? . . ."

By then, having run even a race track, Boston's Suffolk Downs, Veeck was near the end of an athletic journey in which St. Louis was really his only failure. Sure, he almost doubled the Browns' attendance in 1952, but it was only to 518,796, and he liked to spend money even more than make it. Besides, cockily, he couldn't run the Cardinals out of town, particularly when Fred Saigh sold the ball club to Anheuser-Busch in the spring of 1953.

When the public learned that Veeck had cast loving eyes at his old minor-league habitat Milwaukee, which gallantly had built a new stadium on an if-coming basis, the National League beat him to the majors' first franchise shift in 51 years. The Boston Braves, whose own franchise had dipped to $270,000, "owned" minor-league territory in Milwaukee with the Brewers. The NL heeded the Braves' plea and approved the shift on March 18, 1953.

The diamond's domino theory followed: in rapid succession through 1957, let alone expansion later, Boston, St. Louis, Philadelphia, New York and Brooklyn lost franchises, and Milwaukee, Baltimore, Kansas City, San Francisco and Los Angeles obtained them.

Ironically, yet predictably, Bill Veeck was left out, frozen like a lame duck in St. Louis when he shifted his affections to Baltimore. The American League gleefully rejected his application, forcing him to writhe on the spit. The Browns couldn't move for a year (1954), not until Veeck and associates sold.

Veeck was out until he and his ever-changing faithful group bought the White Sox the first time around in 1959, just in time to celebrate a pennant. After an exile due to near-fatal seizures, hardly unlikely in view of his fast physical track record, he saved the White Sox from a possible transfer to Seattle the second time around, 1976.

Veeck would sell for a handsome profit in 1980, aware that player depreciation had run out for tax purposes and the financial doubleheader dip of free agency and inflation were spiraling costs crazily. By then, short a leg, a lung, and half his hearing, with only one legal eye, Veeck quipped, "I figure I've given the world as much of an edge as I'm going to give it."

He would have loved to buy his first love, the Cubs, but he had ruffled the Wrigley family feathers too often. So he stumped daily into the bleachers "with the other bums," sunning himself, often shirtless, sipping beer and exchanging stories with other fans until his death at 72 in early 1986.

The story they wanted most from Veeck?

Why, the midget, of course.

As Fishel recalled, "Bill was happy Eddie had made money out of that appearance in '51. Every time Bill told the story, it went up—$12,000 to $15,000—from national television shows and other appearances. But he was sorry Gaedel was gone."

Of the men mentioned in this tale, too many are gone—Zack Taylor, the Browns' manager; Bill Durney, the traveling secretary; Ed Hurley, the umpire; Bob Swift, the Detroit catcher; and Jack January, the St. Louis *Post-Dispatch* photographer who caught the long and short of it with his camera. Ironically, the first to die and the youngest was the midget himself.

Almost ten years after he pranced to first base in 1951, beaten either in or outside a bar near the Chicago home he shared with his mother, the midget managed to get home and crawl into bed. His mother found him dead the next morning, June 18, 1961. Despite his injuries, a Cook County coroner's jury officially found his death to be of natural causes. A pathologist testified the autopsy showed a heart problem.

At the midget's funeral, only one baseball man was present—the man who had pitched to him. Bob Cain had flown in from Cleveland. A journeyman pitcher for six seasons in the majors, Cain had his best record in 1952, the year he was traded to Veeck's Browns. His 12-10 record included a 1-0 victory over Bob Feller in the lowest-hit game in American League history, a double one-hitter.

Why, I wondered for years, would a player walk—or ride—the last mile for one who had, at least inferentially if not intentionally, humiliated him?

"I owed him that much," said Cain when I reached him, then recently retired. "Because in the many years I've been a goodwill man and speaker for the company, the midget was my best story—before and after he died."

My best story, too.

"I'M GONNA MAKE HISTORY"

Jerry D. Lewis

LEFT-HANDED PITCHERS have a reputation for being flaky. But left-handers by no means have a monopoly on zaniness. After citing Dizzy Dean and a few other right-handed pitchers whose elevators didn't always go to the top, you must consider a pitcher named Bobo Holloman. A rifle arm and unswerving confidence made Holloman a *bonafide* character. A character, however, who would make major-league history in 1953.

"We were still in training camp," recalls Holloman's former teammate Bob Scheffing. "Holloman had just been brought up from Nashville in 1950. He came in with a gang of other rookies. By the third or fourth day, he'd already seen Manager Frank Frisch explode a half dozen times. Anyway, we came into the clubhouse that day after looking terrible in an exhibition game. Suddenly, Holloman yells:

"'Hey, Frank, I need a clean uniform.'

"I figured steam'd be coming out of Frisch's ears. Instead, he turns and tells Bobo to call the clubhouse boy. Not realizing how close he's just come to stepping on a land mine, Bobo shrugs and says, 'Well, I thought you were the top man around here.' On the way back to the hotel, I asked Bobo why he said it.

"'Well, Frank didn't know me from any of the other guys,' said Holloman, 'and I figured that'd make him remember me.' It sure did. The next day, Frank released him to Shreveport."

Bobo didn't immediately know that Frisch intended to send him back to the minors. When the bus got back to the hotel with Scheffing and the other players that afternoon, Holloman found an urgent phone message. Calling home, he learned that his father had suffered a heart attack and been taken to the hospital.

Bobo located a photographer with a Polaroid camera and took him back out to the ballpark. Getting into his uniform, a clean one this time, he posed for a picture to give his father, who'd always dreamed of seeing Alva make it to the majors.

"This'll show him his dream came true," he told the photographer. Taking a cab out to the Phoenix airport, he caught a flight back home to Georgia. He reached the hospital too late. His father, who had no history of heart trouble, never recovered from the first sign of trouble.

Bobo reported a week late to Shreveport. When he didn't mention his father's death, the club fined him. (He never did like explaining.)

During his second year in baseball, while pitching for Macon, in the lowly Sally League, he found himself on the mound when rain began to fall, accompanied by flashes of lightning. Bobo immediately ran back to the dugout.

"It's not raining that hard," his manager told him. "Go on out there and pitch!"

"Not till it stops," Bobo told him.

"Either go out and pitch, or turn in your uniform," the manager ordered.

Bobo quit. He surely would have been excused, though, if he'd bothered to explain that a few years earlier his younger brother had been struck and killed by lightning.

Since Bobo rated as Macon's best pitcher, he soon found himself reinstated. He wasn't so macho that he feared displaying sentiment. Pitching in Macon, his hometown, he knew that the spectators always included his wife, Nan, and his infant son, Gary. Designating both as his good luck charm, he stopped at the foul line each time he pitched, and scratched their initials in the dirt.

"I put my boy's first," Bobo said, "because NG doesn't sound too lucky."

He must have had more than luck in his corner, for he moved up to Nashville the following year. That's when manager Larry Gilbert gave him his nickname.

"You're big, you've got a strong arm, you like to pitch and you like to talk. You remind me of Bobo Newsom." Bobo Newsom pitched right-handed and thought left-handed in both major leagues from 1929 to 1953, and left an army of managers, coaches, and sportswriters shaking their heads and muttering, "What'd he say?"

It took another pair of good seasons before a big-league club bought Holloman's contract. And even then the sale, in baseball terms, was conditional. The St. Louis Browns purchased Holloman for $25,000. As General Manager Rudie Schaffer recalls, "We paid $10,000 immediately, and agreed to send the other $15,000 if Bobo proved good enough to stay on the roster after May 15th." On that date, all teams had to cut their roster to 25 players. That meant marginally talented players drew pink slips.

Leaving the minor-league Syracuse Chiefs for the big-league St. Louis Browns may sound like moving from the slums to Park Avenue. That notion is as wrong as a $4 bill. The St. Louis Browns remained a major-league franchise only because the rules required the American League to field eight teams. During its grim history, the team had finished in last place or next to last 22 times.

After finishing his 1952 season in Syracuse, Bobo went south to play winter ball in Puerto Rico. But when Bobo heard in January that he was moving back up to the majors, he called Browns' owner Bill Veeck—collect. Bobo opened the conversation by saying: "Hello, Bill! This is Bobo Holloman, your new star pitcher. Get three more as good as me, and we'll win it all."

Veeck remained quiet as Holloman went on to describe his matchless talents. Remembering that call later, Veeck said: "He had charm and he had humor and he had unlimited confidence in himself. As I found out, Bobo could outtalk me, outpester me, and outcon me. When he took up baseball, he missed his true calling." As Veeck described him, Bobo could've made a fortune selling radios to the deaf.

"In spring training games, he was hit harder than our batting practice pitchers," Veeck went on, "and things didn't improve when the season started. Our manager, Marty Marion, brought him into a few games as a relief pitcher. Each time, they bombed him. He was a lot of fun, and I loved him when he was away from the pitcher's mound, but it looked like the only sane thing left for me to do was to write off the $10,000 down payment and hustle him back to Syracuse to get out from under the $15,000 installment."

"As we got into May," Marty Marion recalls, "Bobo had an ERA of 9.00." Pitchers with that kind of an earned run average find it difficult to hook up with a team in Little League. "He knew that if he didn't show something real soon," Marion says, "he'd be back taking those long minor-league bus rides. He kept telling me, 'You're not giving Bobo a chance.

Bobo's not a relief pitcher. Bobo's a great *starting* pitcher. I'm gonna make history. I'll show you. Let me start tomorrow night's game.'

"Finally, I gave him the okay just to get him off my back. The next night came—and it rained. He kept pestering me and a couple days later I told him he could start the next night's game. Came the next night—and it rained again. He never stopped badgering Veeck and me to give him a chance.

"'That's all Bobo wants—a chance. I'm gonna make history,' Holloman kept saying."

Finally, Marion gave him the word again. On the afternoon of May 5, 1953, Bobo learned he'd start the next night's game against the Philadephia Athletics, later transferred to Kansas City and finally to Oakland.

Came the night of May 6. The showers which had fallen on and off during the day had become an on and off drizzle. Veeck told Marion they had to try to play the game, with the Syracuse payoff date only a week away.

En route to the mound before the first inning, Bobo stopped at the foul line and scratched Gary's and Nan's initials into the dirt, as usual, then turned and waved to them, in box seats beside the dugout.

Both Nan and Bobo—and maybe even Gary—knew without discussing it that Bobo now faced the most important game of his career. At his age—28—he had to establish major-league credentials now, or forget the dream.

Bobo retired the first three batters easily. In the second inning, though, A's outfielder big Gus Zernial smashed a drive hooking into the left field corner. Brownie outfielder Jim Dyck took off with the crack of the bat. He dove through the air and, flying parallel to the grass, snared the ball for the third out.

With two out in the Browns' half of the second, Bobo came to bat with his battery mate, Les Moss, on second base. He hit the first pitch into center field to score the catcher and give his club a 1-0 lead.

After Bobo retired the A's in order in the third and fourth, Bill Veeck turned to Bob Fishel, the Browns' director of public relations, sitting beside him in the press box.

"If we keep playing," Veeck said, "these people shouldn't have to pay for this game. Write up an announcement that all rain checks will be good for any game this season."

In the fifth inning, A's right fielder Allie Clark hammered a Holloman fastball. From the sound of the bat hitting the ball, everybody in the park knew it had home run depth. As it neared the fence, it suddenly hooked and curved foul by, at most, a few feet. Clark bounced out on the next pitch. The small crowd breathed a sigh of relief, for those keeping score, or paying attention to the scoreboard, knew that the oversized rookie hadn't allowed a hit.

Up stepped Gus Zernial again. He topped a slow grounder to the left of the mound. Bobo, no gazelle at 210 pounds, leaped to his right and speared the ball. Then came trouble. He couldn't get it out of his glove. When finally he did, the wet ball slipped out of his hand and fell to his feet. The official scorer immediately gave Bobo an error on the play, so the no-hitter remained a possibility.

At this point, Bobo settled down and struck out the next batter. As the top of the fifth inning came to a close, Bob Fishel, later the executive vice president of the American League, shoved a sheet of paper across to Veeck. It contained Fishel's draft of the rain-check announcement Veeck had requested. After reading it, Veeck said, "It's okay, but change the word 'management.' People might think I'm taking myself seriously."

In the top of the sixth inning, the A's may have lost a base hit because Fate figured it owed one to Bobo. A's catcher Joe Astroth topped a ball. It rolled slowly, ever so slowly, down to third base. Third baseman Bob Elliott came in. As the ball rotated slowly, Elliott realized he had no play, for Astroth had already reached first. By now, every fan was holding his breath. At the last possible millisecond, just as the ball came within inches of touching third base, it struck something—a clump of dirt or a pebble—and rolled foul.

Bobo then retired Astroth, so at the end of six innings, the line score for the A's read no hits, no runs, no errors. The Browns, having picked up another three tallies, enjoyed a comfortable four-run lead.

Nine outs to go.

The umps called "time" as another rain-filled cloud slowly drifted over Sportsman's Park, a ball field so in need of repairs that one player suggested they'd have to give it a paint job before it could be condemned.

When play resumed, Bobo handled the A's three up and three down in the seventh. In the bottom half of the so-called lucky inning, the Browns loaded the bases. With two out, Holloman picked up his bat. As he did, pitching coach Harry "The Cat" Brecheen called and walked over beside him.

"Bobo," he said, "you got enough runs to win, and your gas tank is getting low. Strike out, so you don't have to do any running."

"You want Bobo to strike out?!" Holloman asked, as if Brecheen had suggested that the pitcher strike his mother. "When I hit a home run, I can *walk* around the bases."

Instead of a homer, Bobo hit the first pitch for a solid single to center, giving him three runs batted in for the evening, and a 6-0 lead.

In the eighth, Joe Astroth, who had given Bobo trouble all night, came to the plate. He drilled a hard shot right past Holloman and through the middle. As the crowd groaned, shortstop Billy Hunter dove without seeming to have any chance of gloving it. He did, though, then spun completely around and fired to first, nipping Astroth in a bang-bang play.

Three outs to go.

Everybody in the small crowd, including Nan and Gary, stood and kept standing as Bobo went to the mound for the ninth. Bobo, well aware of how close he was to a no-hitter, showed his jitters as he dropped the ball twice while taking his warm-up throws. He walked Elmer Valo, the first batter, in four pitches.

Bob Elliott called "time," and strolled over from third. "Hey, Bobo," he said, trying to take Holloman's mind off the game for a few seconds, "where you goin' to dinner later?"

"Get back over there, Bob," Bobo replied. "I'm gonna strike out the next three."

When he threw the next three pitches wide of the plate to Eddie Joost, making it seven balls in a row, Harry Brecheen jumped out of the dugout and ran to the mound. "You're starting to drop your arm, Bobo! Come straight overhand," he advised, then turned and left.

Holloman threw a strike, then walked Joost on the next pitch. The A's best slugger, switch-hitting Dave Philly, brought his .354 average to the plate. Two A's on base and none out. According to *The Sporting News*, Philly hit a sharp grounder on the first pitch. Second baseman Bob Young backhanded it and pegged to shortstop Hunter, who relayed it to Roy Sievers at first for a quick double play.

Now Valo stood at third, but with two out, everybody relaxed. Everybody except Bobo. "It was nice and cool after all the showers," Marty Marion remembers, "but Bobo had the shakes and the sweat was pouring off him."

A's third baseman Loren Babe, a teammate of Bobo's the year before at Syracuse, came to bat. He walked him, which brought Eddie Robinson, the Philadelphia clean-up hitter, to the plate. Bobo got the first pitch over.

Strike one. Robinson swung at the next pitch. Foul tip into Moss's mitt. Strike two. Moss flashed two fingers. Bobo threw what Moss recalls as Holloman's best curve of the night. Robinson swung and smashed a line drive down the first-base line. Foul by inches.

Moss ran to the mound.

"I was this close to catching a no-hitter once before," he told Holloman, "and I missed. I don't want to miss again. He hit that curve pretty good. He'll be looking for the express. Throw him another curve."

Bobo did.

And the strategy worked. Robinson was fooled. He lifted a soft flyball to right fielder Vic Wertz, who jogged in a few steps and grabbed it.

As the Browns charged out of the dugout and joined their teammates on the field in joyfully pummeling Bobo, a fan who had been keeping score walked past the box where Nan and Gary were hugging each other. Reaching in, the fan tapped Nan with his scorecard, then handed it to her and walked away.

"He never told me his name, or waited for me to thank him," she said during a recent phone conversation. "I've still got it."

Bobo, who'd promised Marty Marion that he'd make history, had kept his word. As Dizzy Dean once said, "It ain't boasting if you can do it." Bobo set a record that one day may be tied, but can never be broken. On that night of May 8, 1953, he became the first pitcher in modern major-league history ever to throw *a no-hitter in his first starting assignment.*

Unfortunately, it proved to be the only complete game of Bobo's big-league career. A couple months later, Veeck sold his contract to a minor-league club for $7,500. Within a year, Bobo found himself passed to lower and lower bush-league teams, until even he had to admit defeat, and enter the 9-to-5 business world.

Nan and Bobo found themselves enjoying a quiet evening at home on May 1, 1987, less than a week short of the no-hitter's 34th anniversary. Suddenly, 62-year-old Alva Lee "Bobo" Holloman suffered a heart attack. Like his father's, Bobo's first seizure came without warning, and proved fatal.

Today, Nan Holloman studies the collection of Bobo's baseball souvenirs, and smiles. "Every time I see these," she says, "they bring back wonderful memories of a wonderful man."

TICKETS TO THE SERIES

Bob Barnett

THE SUMMER I REMEMBER most was 1954, the Eisenhower era, beginning of rock and roll. It was the summer before sixth grade and I was immersed in baseball, playing "utility outfielder" for the American Legion Giants Little League team. Newell, my hometown, had a population of 1,800 and was located in the very top of West Virginia's northern panhandle. Our being part of West Virginia was an 18th century surveyor's mistake that caused a thin sliver of West Virginia to be wedged between Ohio and Pennsylvania.

Because of that strange quirk of geography, we lived in the listening areas for both the Pittsburgh Pirates and Cleveland Indians. Most people in our area were Indian fans because the Indians were winners. But it was only an hour's drive to Pittsburgh, more than three to Cleveland. The logic of an 11-year-old mind demanded loyalty to the closer town—despite the fact that the Pirates were the worst team in baseball. They had one heady seventh place finish in 1951 but otherwise were cellar dwellers from 1950 through 1955. It was tough to get excited about a double play combination of Curt Roberts and Gair Allie.

The 1950s was the decade of the Yankees. They were legendary with Whitey, Mickey, Yogi, Billy Martin, Phil Rizzuto, Hank Bauer, Moose Skowron, Bob Grim, Ed Lopat, Allie Reynolds, and hundreds more. They were power, skill, big city; they were invincible. Eight times in the 1950s they won American League pennants. Meanwhile, the Cleveland Indians served as worthy contenders. Six times during the 1950s they finished as American League bridesmaids, five times to the Yankees. But not in 1954.

That was a great baseball season. The Yankees and Indians, as I recall, battled for the pennant all season. Most of my friends were Indians fans and listened to every game. There were two or three exceptions who played hide and seek after dark with girls. We didn't know why they would want to do that and neither did they; it was just something they were moved to do. Later we understood.

I got caught up in pennant fever. The Pirates were still my team, but it was difficult not to get excited about the Indians. Even my Little League coach was captivated. Normally every Little League team in the area got free tickets to "Little League Day," usually a Sunday doubleheader in Cleveland with a loser like the Washington Senators or Philadelphia Athletics. But somehow our coach talked the American Legion into buying tickets for a crucial, late-season doubleheader with the Yankees. I would like to write that the Indians won both games and moved into first place and eventually on to the pennant. I don't remember who won.

The Indians did keep winning and winning, not because they had great players, but because their players had great seasons. Larry Doby (BA .272, HR 32, RBI 126), Al Rosen (BA .300, HR 24, RBI 102) and Roberto Avila (BA .341, HR 15, RBI 67) had exceptional seasons. Everybody played over their heads but what won it was the pitching. They had 20-game winners in Earley Wynn and Bob Lemon. Mike Garcia won 19, Art Houterman 15, and aging Bob Feller won 13 of 19 starts. Even relief pitcher Don Mossi (who looked ugly on his baseball card) was 6-1 with a 1.94 ERA.

When the pennant race was over the Yankees had won 103 games, good enough for first place in most seasons. But the Indians set a Major League record of 111 wins (111-43) to take the flag. They were a great team having a magic season. A team of destiny.

The World Series matched the Indians with the New York Giants who had beaten the *Boys of Summer* Brooklyn Dodgers by five games but appeared to be nothing spectacular. My friends were overjoyed and predicted an easy series for the "Tribe." And I must admit, I felt it too.

But the real excitement hit when my Uncle Jim announced that he had four box seat tickets to the fourth game of the World Series in Cleveland and asked my dad and I to go with him and my cousin Cindy.

Uncle Jim could always come up with tickets for events in Cleveland. He was in sales with the Weirton Steel Company and had strong ties with the Cleveland steel community. People were always giving him presents—tickets to games, watches, blenders, ties, and even toys. Christmas was a real bonanza at their house. Uncle Jim was always generous. He gave me my first two watches and twenty or thirty neckties, among other things.

He and Cindy picked us up at about 6:00 for the three-hour drive to Cleveland. My cousin Cindy was a princess. An eighth-grader in 1954, she was a junior version of Doris Day: wholesome, pretty, gracious, and modest. Strangely enough, despite being almost perfect, she was fun to be with. She was always considerate and comforting to have around in awkward situations. You only had to follow her lead to do the right thing. "No, thank you, I don't want another one either," I often repeated.

The 1954 World Series was a strange series. The Indians were heavily favored but when Willie Mays made "the" catch of Vic Wertz's almost-sure-RBI-producing hit and journeyman pinch hitter Dusty Rhodes hit a tenth inning home run to win the first game, it seemed as if the Indians' hearts were broken. Two more pinch hits by Rhodes led to Giants victories over the dispirited Tribe. Surely the team who only a week ago had been the greatest team ever could win the fourth game and avoid a sweep.

That World Series game was different from the other games I had seen in Cleveland with my Little League team. The huge double deck Cleveland Stadium was as impressive as always. We usually sat in the far reaches of the second deck in either deep left or right field. Higher than the highest fly ball, and further than the longest home run from the field. The players seemed small. But Uncle Jim's box seats were seven rows from the field, right behind the Indians' dugout.

The box seats gave me a whole new perspective on the game. The players looked huge. The crack of the bat sounded like a rifle shot and the fly balls towered above. Hits that appeared to be going over the fence were caught by the shortstop.

The air was different too. It was warm in the October sun, but the thin warmth of Fall. And there was the smell of leaves, the acrid smell of burning leaves and the moldy smell of decaying leaves. It was a baseball game in the middle of football season.

The traditional bunting which hung from the stands was in color rather than TV newsreel black and white. There was electricity. I can't really remember who I cheered for or even much about the game except, of course, that Cleveland lost 7-4. (I looked it up.) But this game was memorable for an altogether different reason.

Wally Westlake, the Indians right fielder, hit a high pop foul in our direction.

With my weak sense of depth I thought it was going into the upper deck. But it hit three or four rows behind us.

The next thing I knew my father dived head first over the back of our seats . . . and emerged with The Ball. Misplayed by some ham-handed fans, it bounced and then rolled under the seats directly behind us which had been vacated moments ago for a rest room trip. Fate.

My father passed the ball around. To my utter disbelief then offered it to my cousin Cindy. To keep. "What?!" I hissed in a stage whisper loud enough to be heard in the Giants' dugout. "She's a girl!" (Remember, it was the 1950s.)

She looked at me, smiled and said, "No, I don't really want it. Give it to Bob." (I told you she was a princess.)

I almost tore her little finger off taking it from her hand. She smiled anyway.

The rest of the game and the trip home were a blur. I kept the ball in my tweed sport coat pocket and touched it every so often just to make sure it was real.

PERFECTION CHEATS HARVEY HADDIX

Walter Langford

IN BASEBALL'S MODERN HISTORY (starting in 1901) pitchers have thrown nearly 200 no-hit games prior to the 1989 season. If at first blush this sounds like a lot, consider that the total represents the modest average of two-and-one-third no-hitters per season. Or, of the 125,000 games played in the majors in those 88 seasons, only 200 of them were no-hitters. Just about one no-hitter for every 625 games. If no-hitters are most exceptional, perfect games are almost non-existent. History records only 11 examples of such astonishing perfecton since 1901—an average of about one every eight years, or one in 11,350 games. Until May 26, 1959 no pitcher had hurled *more* than nine perfect innings in a game. That was true because all the perfect hurlers had won in regulation time. But southpaw Harvey Haddix would change all that.

On that day, Harvey Haddix woke up in Pittsburgh at 6:00 a.m. with a mild case of the flu. But he and his Pirate teammates took a flight to Milwaukee, where that evening they were to engage the Braves, National League champions the previous two years and at the moment in first place again.

"I didn't feel good," Haddix recalls. "But about the middle of the afternoon I had a hamburger and a milkshake. I went out to the ballpark, still not feeling good. Yet I intended to pitch, no matter what.

"We had a meeting before the game in the clubhouse. I was telling how I was going to pitch those guys. I said I would pitch certain hitters high and tight and others low and away. Our third baseman, Don Hoak, spoke up and said, 'Harv, if you pitch those guys that way, you're going to throw a no-hitter.' That broke up the meeting. We all laughed and went out on the field."

As he took the mound that night in Milwaukee, Harvey Haddix had won three games and lost two since opening day. It was his eighth year in the majors in a 14-year career which began with the St. Louis Cardinals in 1952. The '53 season was to be his best when he won 20 while losing nine for the third-place Cards. In '54 he already had 12 wins on July 1 as he faced the Milwaukee Braves in Milwaukee. Leading 4-1 in the fourth inning, Haddix threw a pitch to Joe Adcock which came back at him faster than he had thrown it. The line drive struck Haddix's left knee and disabled him for weeks. When he came back and tried to pitch, he found that the spring was gone from his left leg. "I had no spring to push off with, and I never threw the same after that. I lost a little bit of everything, really. My control a little bit, my stamina, everything." He finished 1954 with a record of 18-13. Early in 1956 he was traded to the Philadelphia Phillies, and after two seasons there, he went to Cincinnati for a year, then onto the Pirates in '59. Handicapped as he was by the knee problem, Haddix nevertheless remained a canny and courageous pitcher.

On the night of May 26, 1959, Haddix found himself facing Lew Burdette, who—with Warren Spahn—formed the heart of the Braves' pitching corps. Their record at that point in the season was 7-2.

"We got into the ball game," Haddix says, "and there was no doubt about it—I felt lousy. I sucked on throat lozenges the whole game so I wouldn't start coughing while I was out there on the mound. It was a kind of rainy, stormy night. We didn't know whether we were going to play or get rained out. There was lightning in the background and everything."

Haddix may not have felt too good, but from the first he was sharp on the mound. His control was at its best and he got ahead of almost every hitter. In fact, he was behind in the count with only four batters all evening. "I threw mostly fastballs and sliders, and I only went to three-and-two on one man."

The Braves' lineup packed a wallop, with the likes of Eddie Mathews, Hank Aaron, Joe Adcock, Wes Covington, Del Crandall, Andy Pafko, and Johnny Logan. But Haddix worked his way through the batting order without trouble in the first three innings. Logan did hit a sharp liner in the third that shortstop Dick Schofield snared with a leaping catch. That was, in fact, as close as the Braves would come to a base hit for another ten innings.

Haddix admits he was conscious of the no-hitter possibility from the start. "Once before, against Philadelphia, I went to the ninth inning with a no-hitter. Richie Ashburn led off the ninth and broke it up. So I'd been through this thing before. I didn't try for the no-hitter. I just kept right on going—three up and three down till the ninth inning. I remember saying to myself at that point, 'I've been this close before. Now I'm going to go for it.'"

Meanwhile, the Pirate batters were getting to Burdette with some frequency. In the third they banged out three hits but didn't score, thanks to a base-running blunder. In the ninth, they got two hits and had runners on first and third with two out and Bob Skinner at bat. He hit a liner which for a second ignited the Pirate bench, but Adcock at first base was able to grab it for the third out. In all, Pittsburgh collected 12 hits to no avail.

The superstition about not mentioning a no-hitter while it was in progress was still quite strong in those days. Haddix recalls, "Some time late in the ball game I came to bat and I can remember Del Crandall, the Braves' catcher, saying to me, 'Harvey, you've got a pretty good ball game going.' He didn't say the magic word. He just said that, and of course I replied, 'Yeah. I guess I have.' And all the time the big scoreboard right up there in front of me let me know exactly what was going on."

The Milwaukee fans were well aware of what was happening, too. From about the seventh inning on, every time Haddix would take the mound or come to the plate, the fans would give him a standing ovation. "That made me feel pretty good," he acknowledges.

And so they went on through the tenth, eleventh, and twelfth innings. In the eleventh, both Wes Covington and Del Crandall hit towering drives that chased center fielder Bill Virdon all the way to the fence, but he was able to pull them in. (Haddix didn't know it, but when he completed the 11th inning he had set a new record. Back in 1906 Harry McIntire of Brooklyn had a no-hitter against Pittsburgh for 10⅔ innings before losing, 1-0. No one else had reached the same point in a hitless game until Haddix matched it in the eleventh and then went on through the twelfth.)

"It went into the 13th inning," Haddix remembers, "and the first batter up for Milwaukee was Felix Mantilla. He hit the most routine ground ball to third base you could ever want. Don Hoak fielded it easily, looked at the seams on the ball, got it just right, and then threw it into the dirt at first base."

It bounced off the knee of first baseman Rocky Nelson. And the perfect game was gone.

But Haddix's no-hitter was still intact.

Next up was Eddie Mathews, who sacrificed Mantilla to second. Then

Hank Aaron was purposely passed, to set up a force play or a double play. And Joe Adcock came to the plate. Haddix had handled him easily four straight times, twice on strikes and twice on ground balls.

The first pitch to Adcock was a ball. Of the second pitch, Haddix says, "I meant to throw a slider down and away. But I got it a little bit up and out over the plate. It wasn't a bad pitch, it wasn't a good pitch. It was just good enough to hit. And you have to give him credit. He didn't try to pull the ball. He hit it just over the right-center field fence."

Haddix's no-hitter went with it. So did the game, 3-0. What might be called the greatest game ever pitched turned out to be just a loss. Recalling that it was also Adcock's line drive in '54 that permanently impaired Harvey's very promising career, we have to conclude that Lady Luck liked Adcock more than Haddix.*

*Lest you think that Adcock's blow over the outfield fence left the final score of that game at 3-0, there's more to the story. His hit scored Mantilla, of course, with the winning run. But Aaron, thinking the ball had hit the outfield fence, rounded second and then cut across the pitching mound toward the dugout. And Adcock, who went around as far as third, was then called out for passing Hank on the basepaths. Warren Giles, National League president, ruled the next day that Adcock was to be credited with a double and the final score was 1-0. Small consolation for the game little guy who had done what no pitcher had done before.

THE
LONGEST HOME RUN

Mark Gallagher

THE GAME WAS OVER and Mickey Mantle of the New York Yankees sat quietly in the visitor's locker room eating peanuts and saying matter-of-factly, "He threw me a fastball and I belted it." Mantle spoke of his home run off Paul Foytack, a shot that cleared the right field roof in Detroit, a shot that got lost, more or less, for 25 years.

Perhaps if Mantle had talked it up a little more, the great homer of September 10, 1960, might have drawn more study. But self-promotion was never Mickey's style; he let others talk and write about his extraordinary play and legendary clouts. And, so, inattention may have been permitted to subvert baseball's longest homer.

It wasn't just Mantle's modesty that conspired to soft-pedal the Herculean home run. Other factors also intervened. For starters, the Tigers had no reason to publicize Mantle, the star of the hated Yankees. And the Yankees' own drum-beater, Bob Fishel, wasn't with the club in Detroit. Fishel later recalled that he usually made only one trip per season into each American League city and this Detroit trip wasn't the one. Apparently no one else in the Yankee camp was inclined or able to document the length of this Mantle homer.

Fishel measured a few of Mantle's home runs even as the successor to Red Patterson. Patterson, the Yankee publicist who measured Mantle's famous 1953 blast in Washington—the 565-footer that has been considered the longest homer on record—set the precedent for measuring long

Reprinted from New York Yankees 1986 SCOREBOOK & SOUVENIR PRO-GRAM and with permission of Professional Sports Publications, 600 Third Ave., New York, NY, 10016. Used with permission of the New York Yankees.

homers. But Fishel found his press box duties too demanding to be measuring every long home run. Once, Fishel, on returning to the press box after locating the landing spot and measuring a long Mantle homer in Washington, looked up only to see Mantle connecting for another lengthy poke. The winded Fishel was off and running again.

As a matter of fact, Patterson measured only two Mantle homers, the one in Washington and another in St. Louis that wasn't quite as long. But Patterson deserves the credit for being a "tape measure" pioneer, although he actually paced off both wallops. Today Patterson says, "I'm just glad I started something," and adds, chuckling, "with a little help from Mantle."

Actually, by 1960, Mantle's sensational swats had acquired something of a commonplace personality. The fans still loved watching them, but another long Mantle homer wasn't really *news*. Detroit's Tiger Stadium is a good example:

A Ted Williams home run in 1939 was the first fair ball hit over the right field roof, and the feat wasn't duplicated until Mantle poled one over the roof in 1956. Mantle repeated the act in 1958, so the 1960 drive gave him three. Thus, of the first four homers to clear the right field roof in Detroit, three were authored by Mantle.

The distance of Mantle's September 10, 1960 home run was accentuated by Detroit reporters Sam Greene (*The Detroit News*) and Hall Middlesworth (*Detroit Free Press*), but John Drebinger of the *New York Times* in his report failed to feature the roundtripper's length. Overshadowing the distance of any home run, back home in New York at least, was the neck-and-neck pennant fight between the Yankees and Baltimore Orioles.

The Yanks' 5-1 victory over the Tigers on the afternoon of September 10, coupled with an Oriole defeat, moved them into first place by just a half game over the Birds (the Yankees would eventually break the race open on the strength of a 15-game winning streak). Besides, Mantle, his big clout notwithstanding, was just one of three stars in the game. Gil McDougald smacked a pair of solo homers and Bob Turley chucked a four-hitter.

The Yankee win did not come easy. New York took a 2-1 lead into the seventh inning, and with two out, Hector Lopez singled and Roger Maris drew a walk. Mantle stepped to the plate batting left-handed against Foytack, a right-hander off whom Mantle had struck his first roof-clearing shot back in 1956. The Mick took two balls and then unloaded. The ball he crushed to right field climbed higher and higher, leaving the playing field near the 370-foot mark, then clearing the 94-foot-high roof and passing through a light tower atop the roof. The ball deflected off a structural member of the tower and disappeared. Mantle's ball was propelled by Mantle alone, his awesome shot cutting through a crosswind.

Sometime during the game, or shortly thereafter, several Detroit sportswriters, including Edgar Hayes and the late Ed Browalski, journeyed to where they believed Mantle's moonshot came back to earth. They discovered that the ball cleared Trumbull Avenue and landed on a fly in the yard of Brooks Lumber across the street.

Paul Baldwin, a Brooks employee, said he saw where the ball landed and showed the spot to the writers. Hayes says today that the group believed the ball must have traveled 600 feet, but direct measurement was impossible and the writers didn't know how to handle an indirect measurement problem—one where it was not possible to take a tape from home plate to the landing spot.

Two and a half decades later, the measurement problem was readdressed. Dr. Paul E. Susman, a clinical psychologist and long-time Mantle fan (he has examined almost every homer hit by the Mick), became convinced that the staggering force of Mantle's 1960 homer in Detroit was never fully reported. Several eyewitnesses, including Hayes and Browalski (before his untimely death), and the 1960 Tiger broadcast team of Ernie Harwell and George Kell, spoke in breathless tones when Susman interviewed them about the underplayed wallop. Ironically, Foytack didn't even remember it, although he vividly recalled serving the 1956 shot Mantle hit out of the Detroit ballpark.

Susman returned to the Brooks lumberyard in June of 1985, accompanied by Robert H. Schiewe, another Mantle believer and a neighbor of Paul's in northern Illinois. Edgar Hayes, in need of a walker now but still eager to help, met them at he yard and identified the general spot where Mantle's 1960 homer landed. The people at Brooks told Susman that Paul Baldwin, the worker who saw the ball come down, was deceased, but they said another lumberyard worker who had been a friend of Baldwin's, a man named Sam Cameron, was still working there and might be able to help.

Cameron was finally found. Did he know where the Mantle homer landed? Yes. Baldwin had shown him the very spot.

Without hesitation, Cameron took Susman to the spot Baldwin had showed him. Cameron, who joined Brooks in 1953 and has been with the company since except for some military service in the '50s, was sure of the location. He was so sure because the ball landed at the base of a shed in which Baldwin was working. The shed is no longer there—it is the only missing landmark from the 1960 scene—but Cameron remembered exactly where it stood.

Schiewe was in charge of the measurements and calculations. He is a man of some accomplishment. He has played semi-pro baseball and has attended law school, and today he is a Rolls-Royce dealer. But most pertinently, he knows some math and can put the Pythagorean Theorem to work. Schiewe had previously examined the area and, like Susman, came to believe that Mantle's 1960 homer was something special.

All the necessary measurements inside and outside Tiger Stadium were made by Schiewe and Susman. The pair measured both legs of a right triangle, the hypotenuse of which was the path of Mantle's homer, and in this way (by summing the squares of the legs) were able to determine the length of the hypotenuse—or the length of Mantle's homer. Keep in mind that the distance from home plate to the landing point hasn't changed since 1960.

When their work was done, they asserted that Mantle's September 10, 1960 homer went 643 feet! An irrefutable principle of geometry was used, not guesswork like so many of the homers that have been estimated in the past. And the dimensions are still there for anyone to reexamine.

It is revealing to note something written about a Mantle homer hit in Detroit on June 11, 1953, when Mickey hit one that landed atop the right field roof, very near the spot the 1960 fourbagger completely left the ballpark. The next day the *Detroit Free Press* stated: "It is reasonable to assume that if the roof had been 10 feet lower, the ball would have carried on out across Trumbull Avenue to somewhere on the next block. Perhaps it would have beaten the 565-foot Mantle home run at Washington . . ."

The 1985 edition of the *Guiness Book of World Records* states that "the longest home run ever measured" was a 618-footer hit by Dizzy Carlyle in a 1929 minor-league game played in California, and that in a 1919 exhibition game, Babe Ruth socked a 587-foot homer in Tampa, Florida. But *Guiness* concludes: "The longest measured home run in a regular-season major-league game is 565 feet by Mickey Mantle (b. Oct. 20, 1941) for the New York Yankees vs. Washington Senators in Apr. 17, 1953, at Griffith Stadium, Wash., D.C."

It is the Washington homer that demands comparison with the Detroit smash, and there are two striking similarities between them. For one, the landing point for each was set by a single eyewitness. Red Patterson paced off 565 feet in Washington, basing the landing point on the statement of a 10-year-old boy. When Patterson hit to the homes beyond Griffith Stadium, he found this youngster holding a slightly dented American League baseball, and the boy showed Patterson where he found it.

The other similarity between the homers is that both struck objects before descending. No one can tell how hard the ball hit the light tower in Detroit, or even whether the distance was enhanced or diminished because of the contact. And Mantle's Washington homer glanced off a beer sign atop the left field bleachers at Griffith Stadium (Mantle hit this one batting right-handed) before disappearing from Griffith's confines. By the way, the ball was displayed in the lobby at Yankee Stadium for a while and was then donated to the Baseball Hall of Fame. Unfortunately, the Detroit ball can't be found, but it is believed that it was once in Baldwin's possession.

Mantle has said his hardest-hit homer was the one he cracked in a 1963 game at Yankee Stadium against Bill Fischer of the Kansas City A's. This one was still rising when it struck the old facade hanging from the roof. The ball missed leaving the Stadium by inches; no one, not even Mantle, has ever hit a fair ball out of the Stadium. A physicist stated that the ball would have carried between 620 and 700 feet if its trajectory had been unimpeded.

So it could well have beaten out the 1960 Detroit homer. But more importantly, perhaps, the range cited also underlines the plausibility of the newly measured 643-foot drive, the new long-distance mark by no less that 68 feet!

MAZEROSKI THE GREAT

Jim Kaplan

IN ONE OF BASEBALL'S supreme ironies, Bill Mazeroski's greatest moment as a player forever obscured his true greatness as a player. It wasn't the Shot Heard 'Round the World, but it was equally dramatic and more symbolic than the celebrated Bobby Thomson hit. On October 13, 1960, Mazeroski, the Pittsburgh Pirate second baseman, socked a ninth-inning homer over the brick wall 406 feet from home plate in Forbes Field and beat the Yankees 10-9 in the seventh game of the World Series. Waving his cap in circles, Mazeroski had to fight his way through crowds to round the bases. Elsewhere in Pittsburgh, people snake-danced down the streets and stalled trolleys by throwing tons of paper out windows. Worried police closed bridges and tunnels. Swamped hotel managers shut their lobbies. Finally breaking away from the celebration, the quiet hero grabbed his wife and ran off to a Pittsburgh hill to sit still for a few moments and take stock of what had happened.

Plenty had happened. The only homer ever to end a World Series, Mazeroski's blast also concluded one of the wildest seventh games ever (remember the double-play grounder that hit a pebble and clipped Tony Kubek in the throat?). Maz's swing also ended what many consider the best-played era in baseball history. The majors had integrated in 1947 without altering their two-league, 16-team format; hence, the golden era of 1947–60. In 1961 the American League would add two teams, the Nationals would follow in 1962, and baseball would head down the road to dilution, divisional play, domes, and the designated hitter. Mazeroski's homer would stand symbolically at the peak of baseball history.

But the more he thought about what he'd done, the less delirious Maz became. What a shame, he told friends later, that he'd be remembered for his bat rather than his glove.

That's being modest: It's a shame the greatest defensive second baseman in baseball history should be remembered for a single at bat.

Not that Maz couldn't hit. Playing in a low-average era (1956–72), he batted .260 with 2,016 hits. A good power hitter for a middle infielder, he had at least ten homers six times. A great clutch hitter—his homer won the first game of the '60 Series as well as the last—he had 80 or more runs batted in twice. But his superb fielding forever distinguished him from his peers.

The second baseman is the most underrated player on the field. He routinely averages as many chances per game as his more celebrated running mate, the shortstop. Second basemen, moreover, execute baseball's most critical defensive maneuver—the pivot on most double plays.

"I never worried about anything but catching the ball and throwing it to Maz," says Dick Groat, Mazeroski's shortstop in 1956–62. "He'd make the DP after getting a perfect throw or a terrible one."

"He was as good as I've ever seen at turning the double play," says former Cub shortstop Don Kessinger. "They called him No Hands because he threw so quickly he never seemed to touch the ball."

On one memorable occasion the Pirates were a run ahead of the Astros with one out in the ninth and men on first and third. A Houston player hit a high hopper to shortstop Gene Alley, who made the only play possible and threw to Maz for the force. Girding for extra innings, the Pirates leaned back on the bench and conceded a run. Seconds later they realized the game was over: Maz had relayed to first in time for the DP.

"That was one of the best double plays I ever made," says Mazeroski, 51, who retired from coaching recently after helping Julio Cruz become a fine second baseman at Seattle and Tim Wallach a top third baseman at Montreal. "Everyone wound up on the ground. Alley fell down making the throw, I turned it with my feet in the air, and Donn Clendenon hit the ground stretching for the ball at first. I'm lucky I have such a strong arm. I never had to wind up to throw, and that helped me a lot on the double play."

Mazeroski's best friends on the DP were his powerful right wrist and forearm, which enabled him to relay to first with a quick flip. With nimble and strong legs, the 5'11½", 185-pound Mazeroski could reach the base well ahead of the throw and push off before the runner arrived. A purist, Maz believed that the most efficient way to make the pivot was to go straight at the runner ("any other way lengthens your throw"). He hung in so tough that teammates called him Tree Stump. When an opponent crashed into him, they had to bring out the stretcher—for the runner.

"He was the best second baseman I've ever seen," says Red Sox executive Johnny Pesky, a former shortstop who teamed with Hall-of-Fame second baseman Bobby Doerr in Boston and later coached for the Pirates when Maz was playing. "One night he dropped the ball. The next night he took a hundred grounders and never missed one. 'Hit it to Maz,' we used to say. 'Hit it to Maz.'"

In one of his most spectacular fielding plays Maz ran down a grounder past first, fielded it near the right-field line, and made a turnaround, off-balance throw of some 120 feet to nip the Mets' Speedy Tommie Agee trying to score from second.

Bill Mazeroski's background is Baseball Classic. His first coach was his father (isn't it always like that?); the late Lew Mazeroski was himself a prospect on the verge of a tryout with Cleveland when a lump of hardrock coal smashed his foot in a mining accident. Bill reported to his high school team in Tiltonsville, Ohio as a freshman, and his coach, Al Barazio, called the team together and told him, "I'm going to make a big leaguer out of you."

Like many great second basemen, Maz was switched there from shortstop (by Branch Rickey, of course). Maz also supplied the personal touches we associate with old-fashioned ballplayers. Leaving the church the day he was married, Mazeroski stuck a chaw of tobacco in his cheek. Maz has hunted and golfed and fished in his time; in fact, he's still called Catfish back home.

Major leaguers had other names for him. By the time he made his first All-Star team in 1958, the 21-year-old Mazeroski was already being called Dazzlin' Maz and The Boy Bandit. When the National League took infield practice, stars from both leagues stopped to watch him.

Baseball people love to listen to him, too. If pressed, Maz can discuss his gloves like a jockey describing his tack: "I used only two or three gloves in my career. I'd break in one in practice and use my main one in games. Some guys have a new one every year; you can't get the feel that way. I also used a small glove. When you reached for a ball, it was there. We were already putting the index finger outside the glove in those days. That creates an air pocket. When the ball hits the glove, it's cushioned."

Maz led the National League second basemen in putouts five times, total chances eight, assists a record nine. He holds major-league double play marks by a second baseman for a season (161), career (1,706), and years leading the league (8). His lifetime fielding average of .983 trails only his Pirate successor, Dave Cash (.9836), among National Leaguers. Cash played most of his career on artificial turf; Maz played most of his on what author and ex-pitcher Jim Brosnan described as the league's worst infield.

In the 1983 *Baseball Research Journal*, Jim McMartin created some all-time defensive listings using such factors as league leadership in putouts, assists, and DPs, and the Bill James range factor (putouts and assists divided by games); McMartin's figures established that old number nine was the most efficient middle infielder ever.

There are those who will go further and declare Mazeroski the greatest fielder ever to hang up his spikes. In their highly respected book, *The Hidden Game of Baseball*, John Thorn and Pete Palmer devised an Einsteinian fielding formula for "defensive wins" at every position but pitcher. Maz finished first. (The only active player likely to pass Mazeroski, says Thorn, is St. Louis shortstop Ozzie Smith.)

So why isn't Maz in the Hall? "I don't get carried away about that because I don't know if I belong," he says in his mild way. "I always thought you had to do it all—hit, run, field, throw—to make it."

But isn't it a fact, he was asked, that many players make the Hall on their bats alone? "That's true. Seems it's an offensive place. If I had the records offensively that I do defensively, I'd be in."

The recent enshrinement of Brooks Robinson, Luis Aparicio, and Pee Wee Reese, who were as celebrated for their fielding as their offense, augurs well for the future. "Maybe the tide is starting to turn," Maz says hopefully.

Not fast enough. "It's an absolute disgrace," says Groat, his voice rising to a shout, "that Bill Mazeroski isn't in the Hall of Fame."

OCTOBER'S SHORTSTOP

Donald Hall

AS WE WAITED for the World Series of 1968, most of us concentrated on a match-up of pitchers. Detroit's Dennis McLain, thirty-one and six on the season—the only pitcher to win thirty since Dizzy Dean in 1934—would go against the Cardinals' future Hall-of-Famer Bob Gibson, whose nifty and powerful kick gave him the handsomest motion in baseball. But the match-up fizzled. Gibson pitched very well—three complete games, two and one, with an ERA of 1.67—but McLain lost two, winning only the sixth game when the Tigers came up with ten runs in the third inning. When the favored Cardinals lost in seven games, it was a portly biker named Mickey Lolich who had pitched the Tigers to three victories—with an ERA of 1.67.

Lolich was glorious. But many baseball people felt that the Tigers won because their manager made one of the weirdest strategic moves in baseball history. Mayo Smith switched his center fielder—a 26-year-old in his third full year with the Tigers, high school pitcher turned minor-league outfielder—into baseball's most demanding position outside pitcher and catcher:

Mickey Stanley started all seven games at shortstop.

By 1968 I had lived ten years in Michigan. Gradually I had come around to Detroit's baseball club in its small antiquated beautiful Tiger Stadium—a baseball park as fine as Fenway Park or Wrigley Field, but without the press. (The city of Detroit never gets the press.) My conversion from Brooklyn Dodgers to Detroit Tigers was facilitated by the managerial treachery of a cross-country flight. Gradually, as I took my son to twi-night doubleheaders, I found myself loving, not just *baseball*, which is always there, but a *team* again: my players, my team of destiny. In a two-night doubleheader with Kansas City, we watched a skinny right hander come out of the bullpen, long man in a hopeless cause, and strike out practically everybody, inning after inning: it was the invention of Dennis McLain.

As 1968 began the Tigers seemed to be going nowhere, again—there were extraordinary *holes* in this team, like three-quarters of the infield—but as the season progressed McLain's remarkable pitching combined with strong help from the bullpen, and Gates Brown became the universe's most consistent pinchhitter: the 1968 Tigers won twenty-seven games in their *last* at bat. They won the pennant pulling away.

And Mayo Smith had a problem.

Ray Oyler who was regular shortstop hit .135 for the season. A more troublesome problem was the status of Al Kaline, who had played 15 years for the Tigers, jumping from his Baltimore high school to the American League in 1953, without ever playing in a World Series. (As it turned out, 1968 would be his only chance.) The 33-year-old right fielder contributed relatively little to the Tigers' great year. He broke his arm in May and the young outfield took over. The Boys from Syracuse, where the Tigers played Triple-A, were Willie Horton in left, Mickey Stanley in center, and Jim Northrup in right. Northrup, who led the team with ninety runs batted in, had a penchant for the grand slam; he hit four during the season and one in the Series. Horton hit thirty-six home runs during the regular season. Stanley hit only .259, but drove in 60 runs; in addition, Stanley played the best defensive center field in the major leagues. When Kaline returned Smith hesitated to bench any of his young outfielders; he played some first base while Norm Cash slumped; then Cash started hitting, .333 from July 27th to the end of the season. Now Kaline became almost a utility man; his hitting suffered and when he dropped a fly ball at Tiger Stadium in August he heard boos. The first time.

Yet it was unthinkable to bench his bat for the Series. Who would sit down? Smith gave some thought to substituting Kaline for Don Wert at third base. Wert hit a mere .200 (how many teams have won pennants when two regular players combined to hit .175?) but he was a solid defensive player. The Cardinals were *fast*—and if Kaline played third the Cardinals would surely bunt him into the grave.

It was the late Norm Cash who suggested that Mayo Smith move Mickey Stanley from center field to shortstop. Now Cash and his manager

did not get on; first base was an open job as long as Mayo managed, and
Cash's opinion of Smith's brainpower was available to the public. Yet when
Cash spoke his piece about Stanley—"He can play shortstop"—Smith lis-
tened. Of course it was general knowledge, as Bill Freehan put it, that
Mickey Stanley was "the best all-around athlete we've got."

However, it takes more than a talented body to play shortstop. Few
people except coaches and groundskeepers and Norman Cash knew that
Mickey Stanley, all season long, took thousands of grounders at shortstop
before batting practice. He was twenty-six years old, intense, nervous, and
every day the first ballplayer to arrive at the park. When someone showed
up who would hit fungos, Stanley worked out taking grounders. He was not
auditioning—Mickey Stanley loved center field—but burning up excess
energy and enjoying himself: he *loved* to play. When Cash strolled out to
first base, among the earlybirds, he watched Stanley siphon grounders and
felt the sting of Stanley's arm.

During the Tigers' remarkable season, Smith (conservative or not) had
been forced several times to switch positions. The day after Kaline broke
his arm, Bill Freehan ended the game in right field. From time to time, first
base was occupied not by Cash but by Freehan, Kaline, or Stanley. Mid-
season the Tigers suffered what someone called "an acute infield shortage."
Tommy Matchick owed weekends to the Army Reserve and Dick McAuliffe
was suspended for fighting Tommy John in vigorous protest over some
headhunting. With McAuliffe and Matchick both unavailable for an
August doubleheader, Stanley ended the first game coming in from center
field to play shortstop when Oyler departed for a pinchhitter. In the second
game Stanley started at second base, the fifth Tiger to play the position
that season. Once Mickey Lolich pinch hit; another time Denny McLain
was a pinch runner.

One week before the Series, Smith made up his mind to play Kaline in
his familiar right field, bench Oyler, play Northrup in center, and move
Stanley from center field to shortstop. For practice, Stanley started at
shortstop the last six games of the regular season. In his first game at
Baltimore he made two errors. But he also made, not a scorekeeper's error,
but a novice's mistake: throwing to first base to complete a double play, he
stood there while Don Buford barrelled into him. (When you play around,
taking infield before a game, you don't dodge spikes.) That night Stanley
called at Mayo Smith's hotel room. "I asked him if he was sure that this was

what he wanted. 'I'm not worried for me; I'm worried for the other players.' He said, 'I know you can do the job; that's good enough for me.' He said, 'You are my shortstop.' It sounded as if, even if I made ten errors those last five or six games, he was going to start me at shortstop. I admired that."

Ernie Harwell, who has been broadcasting baseball for Detroit since 1960, remains to this day astonished by Mayo Smith's decision, because of all the managers Harwell had studied, Smith was the most conservative, the most bound by The Book—that great unwritten tome of probabilities and conventions. In baseball's received wisdom, you *do not switch positions when the game is on the line.* An authoritative spokesman for this opinion is John McGraw who tells us, "When you shift a man from where he belongs, to strengthen another position, you weaken yourself in both spots." Ray Oyler might hit .135 but he knew what a shortstop knows: to go in the hole, to set himself to throw, when to charge and when to lay back, when to cheat, what bag to cover. Although Northrup was a competent center fielder, he was no Mickey Stanley in getting to a fly ball or in hitting the cut-off man. When Ernie Harwell before the Series asked opinions from more than 20 old-timers, he found not *one* who approved of Mickey Stanley playing shortstop. Arthur Dailey summed it up in the New York *Times:* Stanley's "credentials must be suspect."

As the Series came closer the buzzing over Smith's decision grew louder. No position-switch so eccentric had ever been tried in a World Series. A manager might realign the order of his pitchers, and Curt Davis start instead of Whitlow Wyatt; or Jim Konstanty might come out of the bullpen to start the Series—but to play an amateur shortstop was another order of the unexpected.

Skeptical press-noises were nothing to the noises inside Mickey Stanley's head; he was not a phlegmatic sort. The night before opening in St. Louis, he borrowed a sleeping pill from his wife; in the morning he popped a tranquilizer; then, before the game, he vomited anyway. "I suppose," he told Red Smith, "the first damn ball will be hit to me."

It was.

He gobbled Lou Brock's grounder and although he looked awkward threw him out with ease. Later he handled double plays, tagged base-stealers, and took 31 chances to finish the Series with only two errors, both of them questionable, on balls hit deep in the hole. In the second game he started a difficult double play in the sixth inning that helped Lolich out of trouble and preserved the Tigers' first win. He batted a mere .214, less than his season's .259 but considerably more than .135. In the seven games he made four runs out of two walks and six hits, one a triple. More important, the players who might have been sitting performed as they had to: Jim Northrup averaged only .250 but hit two home runs and with eight ribbies tied Kaline for the most; Kaline hit .379 and Norman Cash .385. (Wert hit only .118—but he committed no errors.)

It was because of these figures that, when the Tigers won, Norman Cash crowed: "I think the whole damn World Series was Mickey Stanley playing shortstop!"

Mickey Stanley stayed with the Tigers, his only club, through 1978. Now he prospers as a manufacturer's representative to the automotive industry. He could have stayed in baseball; the Tigers offered him a manager's job in Class A, or a major-league coach's. But he wanted to see more of his children and to make some money. "The day I got my release, I was out pounding on doors. Back in those days we didn't get much money. It has worked out *real* well." Today he seems as full of nervous energy as he did when he was 26. I arrived at his large and handsome house overlooking Silver Lake in South Lyon (minutes from Ann Arbor, an hour from Detroit) to interview him on a snowy morning in January at seven a.m., the earliest interview I have ever done. When I approached the house I saw Mickey Stanley through a window: he sat in an easy chair, frown-lines gathered, studying a computer printout.

Stanley has put on ten deeply-regretted pounds in the last ten years; the strong lines of his face, lightly sketched in 1968, dig more deeply as he approaches 46; and he is as personable as ever, as polite as the young man who addressed older reporters as "sir" back in 1968.

Stanley played basketball and football as well as baseball in his Grand Rapids high school, which he left in 1961 for a Tiger contract, turning down an athletic scholarship to college. He came up to the Tigers briefly at the end of 1964, briefly a year later, and stayed up in 1966. In high school he had pitched and swung a heavy bat. As a major leaguer his lifetime average was .248 and his hitting never terrified the opposition. His outfield defense, as well as his versatility and amiability, kept him on the roster. In his 15 years wearing a Detroit Tiger uniform, he played 1289 games in the outfield, 94 at first base, 74 at shortstop, 18 at third base, and 4 at second.

He was best in the outfield: he was fast; he studied and cheated and got a good jump; he was a great athlete, gymnast or tumbler, to catch the ball. Jerry Green, who saw it, describes a famous 1968 catch in Chicago: "Stanley ran sixty yards diagonally across right center and made a diving catch of Tom McGraw's drive. He tumbled onto the gravel track, arose and doubled Luis Aparicio at first base." Whenever he slumped at the plate, as he remembers, his defense improved: "You want to stay in the lineup." He worked endlessly on his hitting, especially with batting coach Wally Moses who believed in him. "Wally Moses got me where I was. He went to bat for me." (I like the metaphor.) In 1968, "he said he would get me to bat .260. It hit .259 and Wally lost a case of Canadian Club."

Although I watched his incredible play in the Series, there's at last one subtlety of performance that I lacked the know-how to judge. Although he made only two errors, were there balls he didn't get to, that Oyler might have reached? Mickey Stanley doesn't think so; in those days he was *fast*— as fast as Oyler, as fast as Trammel in later years—though he hastens to assure me that he *knows* he was not Ozzie Smith.

Range was not a problem; what worried him were *the situations*: double plays, steals, bunts, pick-off plays. "But because I played center field, all of that was in front of me all the time." Everything fell into place and he knew what to do: he knew more than he knew he knew. "I went to the right place—because I had seen it happen so many times in front of me." It helped to be surrounded by old hands, Don Wert at third, and "Dick McAuliffe was second-baseman and he kept me loose. He'd laugh and make a joke of it. Which was relaxing."

Twenty years after the fact Mickey Stanley cannot remember his double plays, his tags, his throws. I ask, "Can you remember your errors?"

He laughs. "I remember them vividly! Both of them were balls hit in the hole. One was way back in the grass. I dove, got the ball, rolled over—I was short left field by this time—and then I couldn't find the ball. Javier got to second base." The disinterested Red Smith remained skeptical about the scorers' opinion: "The resident friends who are moonlighting as official scorers charged Stanley with an error on the best play of the Series thus far."

Late in the game that the Tigers won, Oyler returned to shortstop, Stanley to center, and Northrup to left while Willie Horton sat down— which improved defense at three positions. But by the end of the Series, no one was worrying any longer about Mickey Stanley at shortstop.

So why not turn full-time shortstop? Next winter, the Tiger management left Ray Oyler unprotected in the expansion draft and the Seattle Mariners took him. Mickey Stanley found himself penciled in as regular shortstop for the Detroit Tigers in 1969. Although he enjoyed center field, "I was really looking forward to that: to start a new career, playing short-stop." And there was another reason: "I thought I could make more money: a .250 hitter playing shortstop is more valuable than a .250 hitter playing center field."

But he hurt his arm; a shortstop's arm is even more crucial than a center fielder's: "I went to spring training; Being young and not *too* intelli-gent, I . . . well, the first ground ball of spring training was hit to me in the hole. It was the first fungo that Dick Tracewski hit—not because he *tried* to hit it in the hole; in was *his* first fungo of the spring!—and instead of fielding the ball clean, getting planted, and throwing the ball gently to first, I had to make a foolish low off-balance throw.

"I hurt my arm.. My arm was never the same. I didn't play a game all spring training, because of my arm, and when I was opening day shortstop, I couldn't throw. I spent the rest of my career with a sore arm, with a bad arm. I *really, really* hurt my career with that throw. I don't know how I lasted 15 years. When I moved back to the outfield . . . nobody used to, *ever*, run on me . . . now, sometimes, people took chances. That was embarrassing."

The World Series of 1968, when he played shortstop and saved the day, was the biggest thrill of Mickey Stanley's baseball life; and it was virtually the *last* thrill: he played ten posthumous years in the major leagues. Fifty-nine games at shortstop in 1969 showed him that he could not do the job. Acquired from the Yankees, Tom Tresh took over at short and Stanley moved back to center field. As a center fielder he tried to fake out the opposition, not to let them recognize how bad his arm was. He also tried to conceal the damage from his own management. "Were they going to release me because I was not throwing at anything close to major-league standards? *Constant pressure*. I felt fortunate to play the next years . . . I could still go *catch* the ball! How many guys does a center fielder throw out? If you use your head and charge the ball, cut down on the distance between outfield and infield, by being aggressive . . .

"I *knew* how different my arm was. Maybe others didn't know. I didn't advertise it. Every day when infield was practicing and outfielders were taking their positions, I would not line up in my normal position, but about thirty feet in . . . I did everything I could to keep people from noticing."

Our conversation slows, as he remembers anxious years. I say that it doesn't sound like much fun.

"It wasn't fun. When all you've done for 20 years is throw, and that's your biggest asset, and you lose that. . . . The last years were not good. . . . 'When are they going to release me?'"

A manufacturer's representative needs many attributes but not a rifle for a right arm. Mickey Stanley enjoys his new life and his work. Still, I get the notion that this morning he is anxious to get started, to drive to Grand Rapids, talk business, take orders . . .

Talking about the last ten worrisome years of baseball, he has entered a blue place in his life. He doesn't want to leave me there. As I rise to go, I can feel him searching for something brighter to send me off with.

"The thing that really helped me," he supplies, "was that Lou Brock took advantage of the situation. Or *tried* to. There is not a doubt in my mind that he was trying to hit the first ball toward shortstop. With a half swing he hit it my way. It had a nice big hop and I threw him out and that took off a *lot* of the pressure."

This notion surprises me; I had never thought of Brock hitting toward the novice shortstop by design. "How do you know he was doing it on purpose?"

"There is no doubt in my mind. He takes a *good* swing at the ball." Then he corrects his present tense—as we stand in his opulent house, moving toward the door, and eight a.m. dawn turns the snow blue, two decades after a nauseated 26-year-old handled a ground ball—and continues, "He hit home runs. He was just doing a little punch job over there. Now if he had waited for five or six innings, and the bases were loaded, things might have been different!"

CONTRIBUTORS

MARK ALVAREZ ("Ruth's First Rival") has authored *The Official Baseball Hall of Fame Answer Book* (Simon & Schuster), *The Old Ball Game* (Redefinition), and a soon-to-be published children's biography of Jackie Robinson. His work has appeared in *Sports Heritage, The National Pastime,* and *The New York Times.* He lives in Woodbury, CT.

JAMES BANKES ("The Magnificent Pittsburgh Crawfords") was, or still is, well-acquainted with Cool Papa Bell, Satchel Paige, and Judy Johnson. Bankes' articles have appeared in *St. Louis Magazine, Baseball History,* and *Sports History.* He is currently working on a series of TV documentaries devoted to the history of baseball. Bankes lives in Sheridan, WY.

BOB BARNETT ("Tickets to the Series") is a professor in the Division of Health, Physical Education and Recreation at Marshall University in Huntington, West Virginia. Barnett teaches courses in sport history, and his most recent work has appeared in *The Saturday Evening Post* and the *Washington Post.*

BOB BROEG ("Chick Hafey's Heartaches," "Veeck and the Midget") was the first sportswriter to earn the University of Missouri Journalism Medal (1971); he later received the Baseball Hall of Fame's writing award in 1979. Broeg joined the *St. Louis Post-Dispatch* in 1945 and continues to contribute sports coverage. He is currently a member of the Hall of Fame's board of directors and its Veterans Committee.

BILL CHASTAIN ("Cool Papa Bell") is a freelance writer based in Tampa, Florida. His baseball articles have appeared in *Sport, Baseball Digest,* and

Sports History. Chastain was formerly the magazine editor of *Florida Sports,* and a sportswriter for the St. Petersburg *Times* and *Evening Independent.*

ED "DUTCH" DOYLE ("Sandlot Babe") spent 22 years as a teacher at St. Joseph's Preparatory School (Philadelphia), where he also coached baseball and basketball. Still a resident of Philadelphia, Doyle enjoys writing and speaking about baseball.

BOB FULTON ("Trip to the Big Leagues") is currently the sports editor of the *Indiana Gazette.* His articles, several on Pittsburgh Pirates figures, have appeared in *Pennsylvania Magazine, Collegiate Baseball,* and *Sports History.* Fulton lives in Indiana, PA.

DONALD HALL ("October's Shortstop") won the National Book Critics Circle Award in 1988 for his book-length poem, *The One Day.* His baseball writings include *Fathers Playing Catch with Sons* and *Dock Ellis in The Country of Baseball.* In 1989 Hall was elected to the American Academy and Institute of Arts & Sciences. Hall lives and works in Danbury, NH.

JOHN B. HOLWAY has authored six books on baseball, most recently *Josh and Satch* (Meckler). His other titles include *Voices from the Great Black Baseball Leagues, Blackball Stars,* and *Black Diamonds.* Holway also co-authored *The Pitcher* with John Thorn. A resident of Alexandria, Virginia, Holway writes on a variety of subjects, from SABRmetrics to astrology.

JIM KAPLAN ("Mazeroski the Great") is editor of *Baseball Research Journal,* a publication of the Society for American Baseball Research (SABR). A former staff writer for *Sports Illustrated,* Kaplan has written several baseball books, including *Pine-Tarred and Feathered: A Year on the Baseball Beat* (Algonquin/Chapel Hill), *Playing the Field: Why Fielding is the Most Fascinating Art in Major League Baseball* (Algonquin/Chapel Hill). He lives in Northampton, MA.

BILL KLINK ("Our Friend Willie") is a freelance writer living in Arizona. His story of the Pacific Coast League's golden years recently appeared in *Sports History.* Before freelancing, Klink wrote sports for the *Newport News Daily Press* in Virginia.

WALTER LANGFORD ("Perfection Cheats Harry Haddix") was a long-time professor of Modern Languages at Notre Dame. Now retired, he has contributed baseball articles to *Baseball Digest*, *Phillies Report*, and *Baseball Research Journal*, among others. His book, *Legends of Baseball*, was published in 1987. Langford resides in St. Louis.

JERRY D. LEWIS ("'I'm Gonna Make History'") is a retired television writer/producer. Having started his career as a sportswriter in New York in the 1930s, Lewis has enjoyed a life-long association with baseball. He now lives in Palisades Park, California, and occasionally contributes to national magazines such as *Sports Illustrated*.

MICHAEL MORGAN ("Bats and Bayonets") is a frequent contributor of historical articles to publications in the Maryland area. His pieces have appeared in the Baltimore *Evening Sun*, *Maryland Magazine*, and *Baltimore Town Magazine*. Morgan lives in Linthicum, MD.

NORMAN L. MACHT ("The 26-Inning Duel," "Young Art's Invention") was once a minor-league general manager. Now he is a freelance writer living in Greenville, Delaware. With Dick Bartell, Macht authored *Rowdy Richard: A Firsthand Account of the National League Baseball Wars of the 1930s and the Men who fought Them*. Macht is now working on a biography of Connie Mack, and also serves as chairman of the Oral History Committee of the Society for American Baseball Research.

W. G. NICHOLSON ("When Owners Reigned") has written many baseball articles and three books, including *Pete Gray: One-Armed Major Leaguer*. His articles have been published in *Women's Sports*, *Baseball Digest*, and *The Washington Times*, among others. Nicholson teaches and writes in Watertown, CT.

BILL RABINOWITZ ("Wilhoit, the Wichita Wonder") is a sportswriter for the *York Daily Record* in York, Pennsylvania. A recent graduate from both Washington and Northwestern Universities, Rabinowitz saw portions of his senior thesis—how baseball and the St. Louis Cardinals survived the Great Depression and WWII—published in *Baseball History* and *Sports History*.

JOHN ROSENBURG ("Hubbell's Greatest Game") has recently contributed articles to *Sports History* and has authored several books, including the prize-winning *The Story of Baseball* (Random House) and *They Gave Us Baseball* (Stackpole Books). Rosenburg lives in Malvern, PA.

MARK VAN OVERLOOP (".303 in 1930") publishes his own baseball newsletter and contributes to *Inside Sports'* "Numbers" page. A member of the Society for American Baseball Research, Van Overloop resides in Washingtonville, NY.

WILLIAM N. WALLACE ("The Judge and I") has been a sportswriter for New York papers for 40 years, the last 26 with *The New York Times.* His first newspaper job was with the *World Telegram & Sun,* his next with the *Herald Tribune;* both are now long defunct. Wallace has written about all kinds of sports in both book and article form; he now lives in Westport, CT.

PETER WALLAN ("Old Hoss") is an unreconstructed Boston Braves fan who, paradoxically, spends his summers as the beat writer for the *Brockton Enterprise,* covering the Boston Red Sox' farm team, the Pawtucket Red Sox. The "PawSox" play their home games a stone's throw from the site of Old Hoss' greatest feats. Wallan is researching New England's semi-pro town teams and factory teams of the early 1900s. He resides in Sharon, MA.